Talking up a Storm

nine women and consciousness-raising

Talking up a Storm

nine women and consciousness-raising

Kristin Henry & Marlene Derlet

Hale & Iremonger

© 1993 Kristin Henry and Marlene Derlet

This book is copyright. Apart from any fair dealing for the purposes of study, research, criticism, review, or as otherwise permitted under the Copyright Act, no part may be reproduced by any process without written permission. Inquiries should be made to the publisher.

Typeset, printed & bound by
Southwood Press Pty Limited
80–92 Chapel Street, Marrickville, NSW

For the publisher
Hale & Iremonger Pty Limited
GPO Box 2552, Sydney, NSW

National Library of Australia Cataloguing-in-publication entry

Henry, Kristin, 1947–

Talking up a storm.

Bibliography.
ISBN 0 86806 504 8.

1. Feminism — Australia. 2. Women — Australia — Social conditions.
I. Derlet, Marlene, 1936– . II. Title.

305.40994

Front cover: Original illustration by Gaye Chapman

Contents

Acknowledgements	*vii*
Foreword *Jocelynne A. Scutt*	*ix*

Introduction
The History	*1*
The Method	*4*

1 THE WOMEN
Bernadette	*9*
Agnes	*10*
Helen	*10*
Rita	*11*
Gloria	*12*
Jane	*13*
Sue	*14*
Rose	*15*
Sophia	*15*

2 THE OLD DAYS

In which the women discuss: Germaine Greer; those Whitlam years; sex, work, friendship; what kind of women did CR; what we'd be when we grew up; parents and husbands; divisions in the movement; what the men got out of women's lib; IVF; single women; childcare; being part of history, and much more.

Interview 1: Gloria, Helen, Rita and Agnes	*17*
Interview 2: Bernadette, Helen and Agnes	*48*

Interview 3: Sophia, Sue and Jane   61
Interview 4: Rose   81
Notes   84

3 HOW THINGS HAVE CHANGED

In which the women discuss: new partners; old expectations; independence; communication; balance of power; stepfathers; retirement; women-only events; women friends; the sensitive male; fear; ageing and ageism; achievement; authority figures; abortion; money, and much more.

Interview 1: Rita, Gloria, Helen and Agnes   91
Interview 2: Bernadette, Sue, Helen, Jane, Sophia
and Agnes   119
Interview 3: Rose   146
Notes   150

4 WHAT THINGS LOOK LIKE FROM HERE

In which the women discuss: the reunion as a mirror; the 'blancmange' of before; the '70s context; did we win the war?; the case of the disappearing movement; mid-life crisis; legislation and reality; today's issues; why did we stop?; memory; sisterhood; being in a book, and much more.

    Bernadette   160
    Sophia   164
    Jane   167
    Sue   169
    Agnes   171
    Rose   174
    Gloria   176
    Helen   181
    Notes   183

Conclusion   189

Bibliography   191
The Authors   193

Acknowledgements

We wish to thank the women of our old consciousness-raising group for their courage, honesty and co-operation.

Thanks must go to Bon Hull for donating invaluable material to the Women's Liberation Switchboard Archives, and Jean Taylor for helping us access those archives, as well as giving us other important information on Women's Liberation. Thanks to Val Byth for information on the Women's Electoral Lobby.

Thanks to Bev Roberts for thinking the book was a good idea in the first place, to Erica Wagner, Carmel Bird, Kate Lion and Sherryl Clark for their encouragement and advice.

A special thanks to Director Rose Goode and actors Kerreen Ely-Harper, Andy Howard, Penny Schlam, Sue Bryce, Anita Rasa, Jane Murdoch, and Claudia Stern for bringing all the words back to life.

Finally, we would like to express our great appreciation to our partners and children for three years of support and patience, and for politely minding their own business while we got on with our work.

Foreword

Raising Consciousness: The Politics of the Personal

In 'Freedom from Unreal Loyalties' historian and artist Sue Bellamy writes of her 1970s awakening to feminism as years that were not easy to live through:

> My life suddenly had different levels of experience, impossible to harmonise. There was the living pulsing reality of the meetings, the other women, the visions and inky leaflets — my real new life. Outside those times, I was in tatters. I was writing a history thesis on a scholarship, yet I really wanted to be an artist and writer . . .[1]

Recalling those early days of the 'new' Women's Liberation Movement (which built, so tellingly, on the activism of women in scores of preceding years), Sue Bellamy observes that the tensions of her overfull life finally burst: 'I remember screaming out one night at a meeting: *How can I write history when we're so busy making it!* It was a pivotal moment in my life: a sudden consciousness of being a woman of my time, not on the periphery.'

Sue Bellamy gained her grounding in Women's Liberation in Sydney, New South Wales. The women in *Talking Up a Storm: Nine Women and Consciousness-Raising* recount their experience in Victoria, in the Melbourne movement. They, like Sue Bellamy, acknowledge the sudden impact of the realisation that 'women's issues' were real: indeed, that there was such a notion as 'women's issues', and that they were a part of them. The women in *Talking Up a Storm* recognise the strength of the feeling that was a part of

---

[1] Sue Bellamy, 'Freedom from Unreal Loyalties' in *Different Lives — Reflections on the Women's Movement and Visions of its Future,* J. A. Scutt, editor, 1987, Penguin Books Australia, pp. 188-99, at p. 190.

consciousness-raising: that they were women at the centre of a political movement which was precipitating a change in the way women were regarded and, equally importantly, in the way women regarded themselves.

These women were not alone. They, alongside so many other women, were propelled into groups, and into talking about the personal politics of their lives, as if their lives *counted*.

Women around Australia who had the advantage of access to the writings of women such as Betty Friedan, Germaine Greer, Robin Morgan and Kate Millet recognised the need to talk. To share ideas of their own understanding and a deepening knowledge about themselves.

Like Sue Bellamy, the *Talking Up a Storm* women did not find life 'easy' in their consciousness-raising period. Juggling husbands and partners, children and paidwork or unpaidwork responsibilities, developing desires for career and personal achievement was difficult at any time. A commitment to a 'bunch of women' made the juggling feat even more remarkable. Yet — they did it.

Why?

In the late 1960s and into the early to mid 1970s women came out into the world — looking for something. Looking for — more! More than the place allotted to women. More than a combination of paidwork and unpaidwork in the home. More than husband or partner and children. More than a cultural and social expectation that women would simply *be*: as the women behind every 'great' man; as the tuckshop mother, devoted to her family; as the dutiful daughter, visiting her mother and father regularly; as the *Woman's Weekly* wife, anticipating her husband's every need; as the obedient consumer, debating the whiter-than-whiteness of competing washing powders and the creamier-than-creaminess of facial soap; as the yearly recipient of refrigerator, toaster, ironingboard, washingmachine or vaccum cleaner on Mother's Day.

'We had all decided,' writes Sue Bellamy. 'We were actors, seizing our chance before the moment passed.'

And was the moment 'seized'? How, now, looking back from the 1990s into ourselves of the 1970s, do we see ourselves then, and us now? The women of *Talking Up a Storm* recognise the important part their consciousness-raising group played in their development into the women they are now. Contraception, abortion, violence against women, economic dependence and independence, (un)equal pay were grappled with. Political positions were developed. Confidence grew. And marriages broke up. Partnerships dissolved, for some. Some bore the brunt of (intended) negative masculine responses: 'You're mother's going out to join her lezzie friends, kids. Wave her goodbye.' There was a lack of understanding that women could get together — wanted to get together — to *talk*. Or perhaps that was the problem: those critical of women's involvement in consciousness-raising recognised only too well the revolution that this would make in the lives of 'their' women, and in their own lives. At the same time, some partners and family understood and supported. Or were able to grow through the experience, together with the women.

Consciousness-raising was exposing. Women opened themselves to one another and found links. Women who otherwise might not have become friends did so. Women sometimes crossed class boundaries. Age was not a criterion for joining. Marriage and motherhood did not preclude participation. And contrary to outsiders' accounts of the phenomenon, racial and religious barriers were broken. *Talking Up a Storm* illustrates this well: the women came 'from six different countries, from Catholic, Jewish, Protestant and secular backgrounds'. Twenty years lay between the youngest and oldest member. One participant identified as a lesbian. Each was *angry* about something.

Consciousness-raising has sometimes been criticised as 'middle-class'. Worse, the charge is that it is apolitical. Yet this ignores the power of political action that comes directly out of women's own experience. The strength of the Women's Movement lies, and has for long lain, in the recognition that the personal is intrinsic to our political claims. The women in *Talking Up a Storm* would without the consciousness-raising group which sustained them through the early years of the 1970s (probably) have 'made it': acknowledged their own worth; followed their ambitions; gained satisfaction in their intimate lives; formed long-sustaining friendships. But, like a film on fastforward, membership of their consciousness-raising group brought rewards sooner and, very likely, made them more longlasting. It brought the pain, too, which comes with differences between women who have accepted one another on a deeply committed level. But it also gave and continues to give meaning to 'sisterhood'. As Kristin Henry and Marlene Derlet say: 'What we share has survived distance, difference and time without contact. It's unsentimental, but appears for almost all of us to be unbreakable.'

Both a painful and a joyful experience, 1970s consciousness-raising advanced women's personal and political understanding. Reflecting back, as any process of remembering the past is bound to be, proved for the women in *Talking Up a Storm* to be charged, sometimes, with ambivalence. Yet, ultimately, the experience is recognised for the valuable contribution it made to the lives of the women directly involved, and to women who shared in the political awakening that came to many women in the 1970s.

Talking Up a Storm demonstates in its reflection and rejoicing that sisterhood *is* powerful.

Jocelynne A. Scutt
July 1993

Introduction

The History

In September 1988 Marlene Derlet and I sat drinking cappuccinos in one of Melbourne's huge suburban shopping centres. Two middle-aged women, we discussed ourselves and the state of the world in much the same way as we had done for the past sixteen years. This particular morning, with the most cynical and greedy of decades on the wane, we found ourselves reminiscing about the circumstances that had first brought us together in an era remarkable for its spirit of optimism and social change.

In 1972 Marlene and I, along with seven other women, formed a women's liberation consciousness-raising group. Neither of those expressions is used much anymore. The less specific 'feminism' has replaced 'women's liberation' which somehow never quite shook off its popular image, manufactured by the media, of wild-eyed harridans cavorting around a bonfire fuelled with Playtexes and Maidenforms. So confronting was the concept of women's liberation, which emerged in America in the 1960s and was allied with other movements of the New Left, such as the civil rights and the anti-war movements, that it was necessary for its critics to trivialise it. By the '70s, an acceptable way to demean a woman while keeping a smile on your face was to suggest that she 'sounded like one of those women's libbers'.

Consciousness-raising was the women's liberation movement operating at the grassroots level. It involved weekly meetings of small groups whose members spoke, often for the first time in their lives, about their experiences as women.

Consciousness-raising (CR) has been criticised by its detractors for being a form of therapy for maladjusted individuals, an example of self-indulgence in an era obsessed with self, and even as a traditional ladies' coffee and chat group masquerading as a vehicle for social reform.

In reality consciousness-raising was the cornerstone of the women's liberation movement. By discussing aspects of their lives — their childhoods, their relationships, sexuality, and gender roles — women were able to see that what they considered their individual lot was actually the shared oppression of women, and they could begin to take action to end it.

As Lisa Tuttle says in the *Encyclopedia of Feminism*:

> CR broke down the psychological isolation suffered by women in Western society and created the understanding that the 'personal is political'. It made possible a meaningful analysis of women's situation, based not on abstract ideas, but on shared experiences.

Our group had been one of many groups which met regularly in Melbourne and the surrounding suburbs during the early '70s. There were nine of us. All but one was married with at least one child. One was then living as a lesbian. We ranged in age from nineteen to thirty-nine and only one had any tertiary education at that stage. We came from six different countries, from Catholic, Jewish, Protestant and secular backgrounds. Some of us worked outside the home, most of us didn't. If we thought of ourselves in terms of class, it was generally in relation to how parents or our husbands saw themselves. Each of us was angry about something.

We came together in each other's homes on Monday nights for two and a half years, at first weekly and later fortnightly. In addition we went with each other to marches and demonstrations, lectures and plays, conferences, working bees and various meetings held at the Women's Centre. We saw each other through the births of babies, abortions, failed marriages, nervous breakdowns, new jobs and returns to education. For those two and a half years we confided in, cared for, argued with and learned from each other in ways and depth unprecedented for any of us. In the process, we became politicised and we became aware of our own power.

So, where were they all now? Did they still consider themselves feminists? Where they still angry? Had their 1970s idealism survived the mass recanting of the 1980s? Did they feel disheartened by the feminist backlash, or were they part of it? Did they feel alarmed, as we did, that the next generation of women seemed ignorant of recent women's history, a history that we had all taken part in making?

As Marlene and I ordered our second and our third cups of coffee, an idea was starting to take shape between us. What if we got the old group back together long enough to present these questions to them, and then made a book of their answers? By the time we left the coffee shop we were filled with a sense of responsibility to record our experience, and excited at the prospect of seeing our old friends again.

It took some time to track everybody down. As we had anticipated, they were difficult to find after thirteen years. All of them had changed addresses and in several instances their last names. I had maintained a very limited acquaintance with two whom I had seen no more than a dozen times since the breakup of the group. Similarly, Marlene had initially kept up contact with a couple of women, but had lost touch with them in recent years.

Now we began to wonder how they would regard this intrusion into their present lives with a request to open up and examine their past. Apart from anything else, we realised that reunions make people anxious. What if they had changed too much? What if they hadn't changed enough? This anxiety could be particularly possible for our group, whose members had parted with such high hopes for themselves and for each other. The spotlight we were proposing to shine on them might not be welcome.

As it turned out we need not have worried. Some were certainly surprised to hear from us, but others acted as though we had been together only yesterday. All were enthusiastic about our idea and willing to help us.

It was then that we hit another snag: I lost my nerve. Conflicting definitions of feminism have formed the basis of hundreds of volumes of weighty theory, and an often bitter dialectic within the women's movement. Did we really want to enter that arena? Were we qualified to add yet another book to the list? Would we be dismissed for being too middle class, not politically sound?

This was just one of the times over the next years that I would be especially grateful that Marlene was my partner in this venture. She never had any doubts that we should, and that we would, write this book. It is to her that the credit must go for making sure I lasted the distance from coffee shop to publisher. In going over and over again our reasons for wanting this book, I began to see that we could, for the most part, deliberately avoid the great arguments about who makes the best feminist. We would not side-step the issue so much as refuse to be tripped up by it. After all, this wasn't going to be a book about objective standards or universal truths. It certainly wouldn't have any statistical significance. In fact, this wouldn't even be a book about feminism.

What this book would be is an intensely personal account of a significant time in the lives of nine women, and their assessing its impact on the rest of their lives. It was our story. It was a good story, and nobody else could tell it.

The Method

Extracts from transcripts of taped interviews held during 1989 and 1990 form the major part of this book. Sometimes it was necessary, because of time constraints, to interview a woman by herself, but usually we met in groups of four or more, and the sessions were frequently reminiscent of the old consciousness-raising meetings.

We started the project without much clear thought of how we would ultimately turn our information into a book. While we had no trouble structuring our questions, it was obvious before the first interview that if we also insisted on structured answers we wouldn't get the book we wanted. After experimenting with different ways of arranging the material we finally decided to present it as it had been presented to us. This meant that we let the women respond to a question through their conversation with each other, rather than by answering the question one at a time.

The questions were divided under three broad headings:
- The group
- The intervening years
- What now?

Because we were never all together at any one interview, we repeated each set of questions with different combinations of women. This means that the same question is discussed in as many as three separate places, but we felt that a little repetition was a small price to pay for answers which have the spontaneity and varied perspective of the ones we recorded.

One problem that concerned Marlene and me was how to be both objective interviewer and subjective interviewee. After all, we had been part of the original group and if it was coming together again to discuss itself, we needed to be part of that reflection. At one stage we thought we might save our contribution for a separate chapter. It was even suggested that we let the other women interview us. But neither of these solutions allowed us to portray our role as group members accurately. Finally we decided to circulate printed copies of the questions prior to the meetings. We then selected one of the discussion sessions dealing with each set of questions in which to express our own opinions. Freed from the need to ask questions, we were able to participate fully in answering them.

This solved more than just a problem of logistics. In order for this approach to work we had to relinquish control of the interviews and, to an extent, of their editing. The raison d'être for this book had been our desire to discover how lasting the impact of the women's movement had been on this particular group of women. We had agreed from the beginning that we would embark on the project with open minds, and that we had no wish to manipulate the information we collected. Our decision to conduct the sessions without the guiding hand of an interviewer was like putting our money where our principles were.

A primary concern of all the women was that their anonymity should be preserved. We felt this was easy to ensure, given that those same factors which had made it difficult for us to find the women in the first place would work in our favour to protect them from identification. Where we felt there was any risk of identification we changed minor details, such as names of people and places. Rather than leave out comments which we believed were important, we attributed them to other speakers, being careful not to distort any of their characters.

Their insistence on remaining unidentified was only partly to do with the nature of disclosures in interviews. As much as anything it was a natural reaffirmation of one of the most important undertakings in consciousness-raising: everyone is committed to honesty on the understanding that everyone else is committed to respecting confidentiality.

With one exception, the women responded with the same candour that marked the original CR group. Only one asked us to edit out part of her contribution to the discussion. Though it had never been our intention to actually revive the group, the tacit understanding that we would operate best if we operated on the old ground rules made our job much easier.

We recorded approximately twenty-five hours of conversations, which both Marlene and I transcribed separately. This might seem like duplicating a task, but we found that it was the best way to gain a real understanding of what had happened in the interviews, and we both needed that understanding equally. Also, we heard and interpreted the recordings in slightly different ways at times, so it was necessary that we both worked from the primary source and then discussed it with each other.

Marlene is responsible for the exhaustive research which has gone into the book. Even though we wanted it to be anecdotal, it was necessary for us to see where our group slotted into the Australia of the 1970s, and into the women's liberation movement in Melbourne during those heady days.

Kristin Henry

The women

Bernadette

In her early 20s when she joined the group, Bernadette was a small woman with long dark hair who never wore makeup and always looked people straight in the eye when she talked with them. Perhaps because of this, she always appeared younger than she was.

The women in the group remembered her as honest, earnest and committed to feminism. With her public servant husband she had investigated many of the alternative movements which flourished in the 1970s. They were particularly interested in those concerning education, spirituality, health and non-nuclear families. Bernadette had her first child during the period of the group's meetings, and shortly after it had stopped meeting she divorced.

In the years that followed she continued her search for answers, moving through a succession of politically or philosophically based communal households. Eventually she retreated to the country where she lived in self-imposed isolation with her second child.

When we contacted Bernadette she had recently ended a long unsatisfactory relationship. She now lives with all three of her children and feels proud of the fact that she is independent.

Her idealism has caused her a few scars, and the years of hardship have taken away the look of youthful innocence, but she isn't bitter. Bernadette has a ready sense of humour which she often turns on herself, but she is essentially a serious woman who considers comments and questions carefully, taking her time and searching for the best words with which to make herself understood.

Agnes

Agnes was 25 when she joined the group, a gregarious redhead with green eyes and an infectious laugh. Her first child was a baby when Bernadette invited her to join a CR group that was just being formed. Agnes had gone from being the daughter of unconventional but conservative middle-class parents to being the wife of a conservative upwardly-mobile man, and she was initially reluctant to associate with women with whom she expected to have little in common. Publicly she put her efforts into looking good and acting nice, but privately she was restless and angry about having her individuality stifled. In the group she discovered that this was a condition shared by many other women. Agnes was articulate and thrived on the discussions in meetings, even though she was frightened by the rate at which her values were changing.

Soon after the group ended Agnes separated from her husband and began a new and very different life with her two children. They shared houses with other families, and Agnes went back to school to get her degree.

Today Agnes makes no attempt to hide the grey hair. She appears both more relaxed and more in control than she ever did when the group was together. She has a career she loves and has been living happily for ten years in a relationship which she says keeps her challenged. She insists that she will never get married again; her independence is too important.

Helen

Helen had her 40th birthday just as the group was coming to an end. She wore her dark blonde hair in a pageboy, eschewed makeup for aesthetic rather than political reasons, and favoured neat, practical clothes.

Helen always presented a mixture of outward conservatism and internal radicalism. In the group she often seemed to have evolved personally beyond the point at which most of the others were stuck and struggling. Financially, she and her husband were comfortable. Helen liked herself, and knew what she wanted out of life. When the other women in the group were leaving unsatisfactory marriages Helen was devising strategies for staying in hers without relinquishing control or compromising her principles.

Before the group finished Helen returned to study. Today, looking virtually unchanged except for a few grey hairs which she recently decided not to cover up, she has the career she always wanted. She is still married and has no regrets about the choices she made, especially insofar as they have affected her child. Nevertheless, she says she periodically takes stock of her situation and wouldn't hesitate to change it if it no longer suited her.

Helen's concerns were, and still are, ones of social justice. In the '70s she was informed and angry about the inequality of opportunity between men and women. Now she is disappointed about how little many of the intelligent young women at her university know about the women's movement.

Rita

In 1972 Rita was 28 years old. She had masses of fair curly hair and she chose clothes which were calculated to reveal her voluptuous figure. She was a talented, intelligent woman who, in spite of her obvious attributes, often seemed unsure of herself.

Rita had married in her teens and at the time the group met she had two young children. Her relationship with her artist husband appeared to be built on affection and companionship, but was unorthodox in that both partners tolerated, even encouraged, casual sexual encounters outside the marriage. When one of these developed temporarily into something more serious for Rita the marriage ended. Rita left home and the children stayed with their father.

By this time Rita had begun a course at university. In the following years she managed to gain a degree and a Dip.Ed, and to establish herself as a stage performer. During this period she changed addresses frequently and had a number of disastrous relationships with men. At the time we contacted her she had been in a stable relationship for several years.

On the day of our reunion Rita obviously felt ambivalent about the old group. She stated that she had not wanted the meetings to end. On the other hand she admitted that she had held on to some grievances toward some of the women. She said that there were things about her life that she regretted, and that other people had let her down.

Every now and then Rita would laugh at something, and for a moment her eyes would regain their sparkle and the years would fade from her face. But most of the time she appeared tense, distracted and unhappy.

Gloria

Gloria was a tall dark solidly-built woman in her early 40s. She wore lots of silver bangles and great hoop earrings and had an irrepressible personality. An early school leaver, she resumed her education during the period in which the group was together, and set her heart on becoming a teacher.

This met with resistance from her large wealthy Jewish family, who constantly put pressure on her to give up her studies and concentrate on looking after her house and children, who were then in their late teens. Instead, Gloria left home to live in a small flat. She supported herself financially through TEAS* and emotionally through her contact with other mature-age women at teachers'

---

* Tertiary Education Assistance Scheme, 1974-1986.

college. In the group Gloria had been full of energy and enthusiasm. Some of the women remember her as a kind of role model for guilt-free sensuality. She had the ability to accommodate the shortcomings of others; to acknowledge the negatives but accentuate the positives.

Now in her late 50s Gloria hasn't changed much, either in appearance or outlook. She is a little greyer and a little rounder, but still as full of the joy of life as ever. She lives with her second husband and dotes on her many grandchildren. Her only worry is that she may actually be too happy. She fears becoming complacent and slipping back into the traditional role she discarded years ago. She is still prone to what she calls the 'Jewish family's dutiful daughter syndrome'.

Jane

In the CR group Jane had presented herself as a quiet but capable and self-assured 30-year-old. She looked fresh-faced and healthy. The only daughter in a large working-class family, she had been attracted to the women's movement because of her early exposure to sexism and inequality.

Jane had left her first husband and was working on her bachelor's degree by the time the group ended. She has three older children who live with her and her second husband, whom she married almost immediately after her divorce.

A no-nonsense woman, Jane is sometimes very dryly funny. She now looks every inch the successful business woman, from the hem of her tailored suits to her professionally tipped hair. Yet for someone so much in the mainstream she has an obvious lack of reverence for many of its institutions. One senses Jane's determination to get what she wants out of life, and a pragmatism that serves her well. She has large round eyes which seem to catch and hold anyone she is speaking to and her frank face sometimes hints at a secret amusement.

Apart from that, she is often hard to read. Essentially a private person, Jane rarely volunteers much about her feelings, and can sometimes appear neutral in a discussion, even distant. It comes as a surprise to discover when she does talk that she sees herself as totally involved. For the reunion she had hunted out an old photograph of the group, probably the only one ever taken.

Sue

Sue was 30 and had just had her second child when she joined the CR group. She and Jane were close friends who came to meetings together. Both women were in unhappy marriages to men who were busily working their way up the corporate ladder. The bond the women shared with each other was obviously much stronger than anything either of them had with their husbands. For the rest of the group they had embodied the ideal of friendship between women.

Sue was friendly, funny and outspoken about inequality between the sexes. She had, and still has, blue eyes which act as a barometer for her emotions.

She was also unfulfilled as a wife and sometimes unsure of herself as a mother. Naturally gregarious, Sue enjoyed an active social life but was often in trouble with her husband for making statements which outraged his conservative friends. Eventually he and Sue parted under circumstances which she describes as 'very, very nasty'. Except for a short initial period, both children lived with Sue. What followed was for her a period of humiliating poverty and isolation.

At the time of the reunion Sue had a good job, a classy wardrobe and a new relationship which she insisted was totally different from her marriage, with one exception: she was still expected to do most of the domestic chores. She seemed caught between her old resentment of unfairness and a new found pragmatism. She admitted that loneliness was a big issue for her.

The years have given Sue a calmness and stature without taking away the old earthy humour. She still smiles encouragingly at people when they talk to her.

Rose

In the group Rose had been quiet and good natured, happy to answer questions but rarely volunteering much about herself. She found the group a source of friendship with other women, which was something she had missed since moving to Australia from Scotland.

Rose was a striking woman in her late 30s with great bones and a constantly changing hair colour. She had children in their teens and she worked full time. Her job was important to her, as was her working-class background.

She had been married for a number of years but had also been involved with another man for a long time. She had the ability to compartmentalise the different areas of her life. Her husband hadn't interfered or tried to place any restrictions on her. Rose says if he had she would have left him much earlier.

As it was, she was in the process of getting a divorce when we contacted her. She is still beautiful, and still happy in her work, as in her new relationship. True to form, Rose did more listening than talking at the reunion. What she did say was that at this stage in her life she wants to avoid fights and drama. Also, these days what matters to her differs from what used to matter. She is more interested in her grandchildren than in politics or social issues. It has occurred to her that her new contentment might lead her into stagnation. Nevertheless, she has no desire for any great new experiences.

Sophia

Sophia was a young university student when the group began. Her interest in feminism was at least partly a reaction against the male domination of her southern European family's traditional culture.

So committed was Sophia to the women's movement that for several years her every action, every friendship, was examined for its political implications. Apart from attending weekly CR meetings she devoted a great deal of time to numerous working committees. She virtually excluded men from her personal life, preferring to live with older women whom she saw as role models. In the group she was good humoured but always challenging.

In the old days Sophia had favoured clothes which were not gender specific. So her entrance on the day of the reunion was clearly designed to deliver a message with maximum impact. She arrived late, wearing a tight skirt, stiletto heels and long red fingernails. Her crusading days were over.

She obliged her surprised sisters with a brief account of the changes in her life since the group had disbanded. These included several relationships with men, a reclaiming of the female and artistic parts of herself, and a demanding career. She seemed genuinely pleased to see the other women, but stressed that her feminist zeal had caused her severe burnout, and she had no desire to get involved in a CR group again. She said she doubted that she could contribute much to the project.

2
The old days

In which the women discuss: Germaine Greer; those Whitlam years; sex, work, friendship; what kind of women did CR; what we'd be when we grew up; parents and husbands; divisions in the movement; what the men got out of women's lib; IVF; single women; childcare; being part of history, and much more.

Interview 1: 18 and 19 February 1989
Gloria, Helen, Rita and Agnes

One midsummer weekend several of the women were able to get away to a comfortable holiday house on Phillip Island. With no interruptions, they relaxed and started getting to know each other again.

In the following conversaion they recall what their lives were like before they became involved with the women's movement. They also talk about how they interacted with each other in the group. The objectivity they had acquired over the years added an extra dimension to their memories. Though the interviews were never intended to be consciousness-raising sessions, the women found that they fell easily into a type of communication that was frank and sometimes extremely personal. While the subjects discussed are serious, and the tone is sometimes sad, even angry, there is a great deal of laughter throughout, which would seem to refute the old rumour that feminists have no sense of humour.

On Saturday afternoon we started recording the conversation. We began by asking the women to remember what had led them to join a consciousness-raising group in the first place.

RITA: I remember going to some kind of a hall. It might have been Camberwell, and Ainslie Mears was speaking. And there was also a woman who talked about how in some countries women are . . . it's like being circumcised . . . that's it, clitoridectomy. That memory has been blended into a whole lot of other things. It gets a bit jumbled now. But it was specifically about the study of things that have happened to women . . . the state of women throughout the world.

HELEN: I was always interested in the question of feminism. Perhaps I didn't call it feminism. But I always found, even as a child, that in society the fact that a person was born a male meant he had certain privileges. Right from the beginning. And all my life I found that in discussions males were listened to more, just for the sheer fact of being male. They were considered to be the experts on politics, on philosophy, on everything. Now I always felt this was very wrong. And the thing I always found so unjust was . . .

AGNES: . . . you were smarter than they were.

HELEN: *(laughing)* Yes, that was one thing. But it was that everybody had this perception that men should be deferred to. Even I did. Even when I knew I'd had more education than they had. I'd read more books than most of the ones I knew. So why was it? I just found it so unjust. And of course there were other things, double standards about sex. Men had affairs and they were just being men. We did it and we were being bad. Being a woman had always given me a . . . you know, a second-class feeling. I even had that perception of myself.

GLORIA: You fell for the whole advertising campaign.

HELEN: Yes, exactly. And then Germaine Greer* came here and she was in the papers. She was a witness in an obscenity case for *Oz* magazine in Sydney and some other magazine in Melbourne, but she also did some public speaking. Always before it was men doing the speaking and having the authority, and I thought *That's it. I'm going to listen to her. Why should I accept everything men say? I've done that for years. I want to find out what women have to say.* So that was my reason for going. And when I listened to the women who spoke there . . . I can't even remember what they said . . . I thought this was for me. And that was my start.

GLORIA: You were sort of outward looking. I think I was just sort of so . . . suppressed, you know. And suddenly Germaine Greer was there, and there were articles in the paper and people were talking about it. And I thought *It's not just me!* And I thought I had to know more about it.

AGNES: I realise when I hear you talking now that I never saw myself as part of a large population that was experiencing something. I saw myself as very much an isolated individual. I can remember back to one of the earliest jobs I tried to get, in the days when unless the advertisement said the job was for a female, it was for a male. This was with the Public Service and it was for a clerk, instead of a female clerk. Somebody told me I was wasting my time applying for it. And I thought, *Well, let them tell me that. If I get an interview let them tell me I can't have the job because I'm a girl. Let them tell me that regular means male, and female means irregular.* I was just a kid, but I was qualified for this job, and I got the interview. I sat outside the office on a bench seat with a whole bunch of young men. They hadn't been able to tell from my name because it was unusual in those days. They were shocked when they saw me, and of course it didn't get me anywhere.

I was just angry and wanted to prove a point. But I never saw

---

* Author of *The Female Eunuch*, Paladin, 1970..

my action as an example of women being fed up. And I never thought of myself as a women's liberationist. I didn't have the sort of overview you had. I didn't think of the big picture . . . just the little one.

RITA: I was just thinking that all my life before I joined the group I had the feeling that women were put down and kept back for no good reason, but I never discussed it with anyone because there was no one to talk about it with. Then Germaine Greer's book came out. I'm not saying that was the catalyst to everything for me, but when I read it and saw what she was saying I knew this was the beginning of more widespread things. I hadn't read much about the feminist movement or women's liberation before that. So after I read her book I think I must have rung up the Women's Centre. And then I joined a CR group.

AGNES: Well, Bernadette invited me to go with her to a women's liberation meeting and I just agreed without thinking about it. But it was like buying something from a door-to-door salesman and then regretting it later. The day of the meeting came and I really didn't want to go. I had just had a baby, and my whole life was really just . . . I didn't see beyond the walls of my house. But I couldn't contact Bernadette and I'd arranged to pick her up in my car, so there was nothing for it but to go. Bernadette and I had known each other at school but hardly ever saw each other any more. If it hadn't been for her I would have never gone. Well, I don't know about never, but certainly not then.

RITA: I'd started back at night school around the time I joined the group. I was doing English and Social Studies. So I was reading books, becoming . . . not aware, but having my preconceived ideas actually reinforced.

AGNES: You see? You all sound a lot more politically tuned-in than I was. I never read a newspaper, I never watched television . . . I don't know what I did do! I honestly don't know.

You said you'd always realised women were held back. Well, back then the women I knew would have denied that. Except possibly my mother, and I didn't pay any attention to her because I thought she was a weirdo, and I didn't want to be one myself. *(Here Agnes laughs at the memory of the conspiracy.)* My neighbours, my mother-in-law, my husband's mates' wives . . . all thought, or at least said . . .

RITA: . . . don't rock the boat.

AGNES: Yes. So, I was absolutely convinced that I was a troublemaker if I wasn't satisfied. There was some flaw in me, because all around me there were these happy little women. If there was any problem it was mine. *(Agnes and the others laugh.)* I feel like crying about that now. It makes me angry all over again.

GLORIA: It was like that for me too. I was being told I should be happy because I was doing all the right things. The wife and mother bit. But I knew I wasn't happy. Life was just so miserable. And I had to find out . . . surely this wasn't all there was to it. I was searching but I didn't even know what I was looking for . . . what I wanted.

And I think then, with Germaine Greer and her book and all that was going on when it came out, I started reading. And I realise now, it was like you said, Rita. I phoned the Women's Centre and I asked where a group was close to me. And that's how it started.

HELEN: The Movement came just at the right moment for a lot of women.

RITA: And there were a whole lot of other things going on as well. Like the Labor Party getting in after 23 years in the wilderness. And the books had started coming out. You know, Betty Friedan's book *The Feminine Mystique*.* And people were saying: 'Yes, that's

---

* Penguin, 1963.

right, that's what's really going on.' So it was a real eye-opener for me. It was exciting, that time in the early '70s.

HELEN: Yes, it was very exciting. Politically and every other way. People were committed in those days. They had causes.

AGNES: Nowadays that level of commitment seems like aberrant behaviour. As though we were all fanatics back then and we should feel slightly embarrassed now.

HELEN: I never saw myself as fanatical.

AGNES: No, of course not. But see, commitment is one of those words that belongs back in the '70s, isn't it?

GLORIA: It's not so fashionable now.

AGNES: Right. And that's why fanaticism is a relative concept, you know. If you're committed to nothing, then commitment to anything can sound quite over the top.

HELEN: I was just thinking that there was another difference between me and some of the other women. I never had the dream of being a happy housewife and mother. When I was a teenager I thought of marriage as okay, but not everything. I always saw myself as a writer, or . . . don't laugh . . . a film star. Sometimes as a business woman. I had a husband in there somewhere, because it was the thing you did as a woman. In the '50s women got married. But I only ever saw one child. It was still going to be *my* life. Perhaps that's why I caught on very quickly. I was aware of the injustice because I knew that all I dreamed of I might not be able to do, because I was just a woman.

RITA: Well, I was already married when I was a teenager. But when I was a child I saw my future as an adventure somehow. I was going to be an air hostess or a film star *(Rita laughs apologetically)*, or I was going to ride horses all my life, or I was going to be some kind of a wonderful singer and musician.

GLORIA: Did you see a husband and children in that dream?

RITA: Yes, yes . . . but I sort of pushed them aside a little bit. It wasn't the be all and end all of everything to me. I projected an image of *myself*, more than anything. But of course, I suppose I realised that in this society a woman must be married and have children to be recognised as a proper woman.

HELEN: Perhaps another thing that influenced me was that from the time I was fifteen I was out and travelling. First I was at boarding school and then I rented rooms by myself. Then I went to Italy for a few years and I worked at different jobs so I'd have money to travel. From the time I was nineteen until I met my husband at twenty-three, I travelled alone. Some of those European cities were quite dangerous in those days. I'd go into a restaurant and sit there alone, and there were all these sailors around. They looked at me and saw that I was free, and it was as though I was a wild animal, there to be taken, to be exploited. And I always felt the old injustice again.

GLORIA: And you wouldn't have been there alone unless you wanted something to happen.

RITA: That's still the case. A woman turns up alone in some place and . . . you know . . . the men there think she must be there for them . . . why else? My girlfriend and I go out to different places. There's a piano bar which isn't too bad, but sometimes there are fellows there that think . . . you know . . . they'll do us a favour. We've gone to some places, just to sit and have coffee, have a drink, whatever, and talk about our work or . . . anything. And fellows think we need to be approached. It's so annoying. The arrogance.

At this point the conversation went from lone women in public places to the experience of women who find themselves alone after having been part of a couple. Towards the final days of the CR group and during the period after it disbanded, all of the women except for Helen went through divorces. Here they discuss the reactions of their friends to their change in status.

GLORIA: Yes, friends. I lost a lot of friends. They just didn't invite me to do things with them anymore. Or they phoned me up and asked me over when the husband wasn't there. Just come for lunch . . . you know . . . but no dinner parties.

AGNES: I even got left out of neighbourhood barbecues and things like that. I used to feel so awful for my kids, because they could hear these parties going on over the fence. Everybody else in the street would be invited, and all their mates would be on the other side of that fence. Everybody but us. We were just pariahs.

RITA: No, it was different for me. Of course I didn't keep up associations with my ex-husband's mates but I had other people. When I joined the Labor Party I did a lot with people from that group. And with all of you. And I became involved with the theatre, but that wasn't until later.

HELEN: I think you're talking about a different set of people. They may accept more. But you know . . . Agnes's suburb . . . middle class . . .

AGNES: It was the worst place in the world to be divorced.

HELEN: Well, now I'll tell you my side. I'm probably guilty of not inviting any of you when you were alone. First of all, we aren't party givers, right? We often go out with people, but . . . I feel guilty. I've talked to other women about this and . . . I wasn't scared that you'd get my husband or anything like that. It was just . . . I didn't know how to deal with it. I've learned since then. I've invited a single woman for dinner, and had another couple with us. But, you know . . . we're not inviting people. But I have thought about that. Why didn't I invite you and you? And there were others. I feel uncomfortable.

AGNES: I can think of one reason, and you can tell me if I'm wrong. I'm quite sure your husband disapproved of me because I separated.

The old days

HELEN: Right. I'll say something about this because it might have happened to other women. You see, when you all split up . . .

AGNES: I led the way. *(Agnes laughs with the others at this image of herself.)*

GLORIA: And we were always influencing each other, weren't we. Like a herd of cows. I'm leaving mine, so you leave yours.

HELEN: Yes, well, my husband felt very threatened by all that splitting up, so the first thing of course was that he said: 'Oh, now you'll want to do like Agnes'. And he focused on Agnes, though he liked her very much, but he disapproved very much of her actions. She had a lovely husband, and . . . he just couldn't understand. 'They were always sitting together,' he said. Remember, you were always holding hands and you seemed to be having so much fun. He couldn't understand how you could split up.

And we went through a bad time ourselves around then, and he felt very insecure. He felt that the whole thing was such a threat, and that Agnes was going to influence me. As if I had no mind of my own. I'd just started H.S.C.* and . . . oh, that was a bad time for him. That was one reason. And of course, the other thing was . . . he said to me: 'You're a lesbian, aren't you? You're turning. I always wondered what you did in that group.'

AGNES: Yeah, we had orgies in my lounge room. *(Everybody laughs.)*

HELEN: One day, I think several of us had met, and I came home and said what an interesting day it had been, and he said: 'That's nice.' But then, about a week later we were having a fight and he said: 'Oh, I know what you three lesbians were up to.'

So, of course, I'm not going to invite trouble into my house. I thought, right, the group is mine. You're mine and you're mine and you're mine, and that's it. And always since then I keep my friends to myself and I don't want them to come into the house. I want to

---

* Higher School Certificate, Year 12 in Victorian high schools before 1990.

meet them somewhere else. I don't want snide remarks. Though he's stopped it now. That's past . . . but I'm still very conscious of it.

RITA: It's easy for men to feel threatened by women . . . easy.

AGNES: But let's face it, that was a threatening situation. I mean, most of us were married to nice men, not bastards who beat us up.

HELEN: Right! He could have understood that. That would have been fine. You don't stay with a man who beats you up.

AGNES: But if even nice guys could be walked out on . . . kind men, good fathers, good providers . . . well, something had to be wrong with the women. We all had to be either whores or lesbians. If ordinary women could do it . . . just because they weren't happy . . . his own wife could do it to him.

HELEN: Well, that was the situation. I knew that eventually it would come back to me. Somehow I was going to suffer because you all left your husbands.

GLORIA: Poor Helen!

RITA: When you're a single woman who has been married, living in a house with your children, you suddenly become depraved. I remember going to different functions and meetings of organisations that I belonged to. And there was this one man who had shown an interest in me . . . you know, spoken nicely to me . . . and then suddenly when I was without my husband he became more and more interested. He was living with his wife and children at the time. And some of the other people in the organisation started talking about me, and what a terrible person I was. Nothing about him, just what I was doing to his marriage.

GLORIA: That's important, because it's an example of how women are fair game, and also of how they're the ones that get blamed.

AGNES: Also, some men made assumptions about what was going

to be in it for them now that women were suddenly getting 'liberated'. I remember having coffee with this guy who sat there trying to appeal to my . . . liberated spirit, you know. Tried to flatter me that I was the New Woman who didn't have all those old-fashioned hangups . . . so how about it? But it was my inhibitions I'd given up, not my discrimination, and not my right to choose. I was so angry with him. He was one of the smart ones who was quickly going to start changing his seduction line because the old one probably wouldn't work with this type of woman. Now he was going to say: 'Look, I'm totally in tune with what you're doing. I think it's fabulous. So let's party.' *(There was a great deal of bitter laughter as the women remembered their own examples of this opportunism.)*

RITA: Yes, it's the same old bottom line. Just the approach is changed.

GLORIA: Yes, a variation on 'I'll do you a favour'.

HELEN: It's interesting how quick some men were to try to exploit women's liberation. They misinterpreted the whole thing.

GLORIA: They thought, 'This is great. Now I don't have to tell her I love her. We can just get straight into bed'.

HELEN: So, can men really be feminists? I haven't come across any. Somehow I just can't believe it.

RITA: Not when they feel that the only way they can be real men is if they can talk some woman into going home and sleeping with them. People say that's just the way men are . . . they get a thrill out of having one-night stands, blah, blah, blah. Okay. But some women like that too, so I think there's a lot more to it than the sex. I think the reason men attach so much importance to 'getting around' women is because they see *that* as the real conquest. Not the sex, but the seduction itself. That's what makes them a man. You know what I mean? The important thing is not the sexual thrill, it's the thrill of pulling the wool over her eyes, which is really about exercising power.

AGNES: This is one reason why I value my friendships with gay men. That stuff just doesn't come into the relationship, so we're able to really know each other and talk to each other. They've already decided that they won't be measuring their manliness in terms of how many women they can score with. They have different ways of valuing themselves.

We were interested in finding out how the husbands of these women had felt about their wives becoming involved with women's liberation.

GLORIA: Oh, I think my husband just thought we were going to exchange recipes. He had no idea, and he probably also thought that with me it wouldn't last long anyway . . . that it was just another new thing I'd found and after a while I'd go off and do something else.

RITA: No, my husband was actually quite behind me. I mean, he thought that I could learn a lot. He was aware of what it was all about. He was really quite supportive.

HELEN: Actually, mine was too. I mean, he never has much choice with me anyway once I make up my mind. But he was quite supportive. He said I should go and that I might find it very interesting because I like political things. But, I'm still questioning the motives. He had a very demanding job. He was practically working all day and night. And he's said to me since that he couldn't have worked like that if I hadn't been doing my own thing. He was worried that I'd get bored.

AGNES: Well, I thought that my husband never took anything I did terribly seriously. In fairness, he might say that's not true. But you know, if I'd said I wanted to join a pottery class, that would have been fine too. In his family the women learned to value themselves according to how well they cleaned and cooked and stuff like that.

His family used to talk about me as though I was sort of a novelty item . . . they used to say things like: 'Agnes is very intelligent'.

RITA: I can hear it: 'This is Agnes. She's intelligent'.

AGNES: Yes. And he seemed to think I was okay . . . not really what he'd planned to marry though. There were these extra bits that he didn't know what to do with . . . but he was very kind to me. And he probably thought if I could go and talk to some other women it might keep me from being unhappy. Because he did know that I was unhappy . . . he just didn't know why. Maybe he thought the group would be able to cheer me up.

HELEN: I often feel that this is the attitude I get in conversations with men. They listen to you just to keep you happy and then they go on with their big business that only they understand.

AGNES: No, it wasn't like that. He may not have understood, but he took it seriously. I remember about a year after we started the group. I was going out to a meeting one night and . . . bear in mind that we never confronted each other with anything serious, ever . . . and he stood in the door and he said: 'Something's happening to you and I can tell that I'm not going to be able to stop it'. And he said: 'I don't know whether I would if I could, but I know I can't. And I don't know where it's going to take you, and I don't know what it's going to mean to me'.

GLORIA: That was quite a profound insight.

AGNES: Yes, especially for somebody like him. He'd realised it wasn't the ladies' coffee evening . . . it was something that was going to have very far-reaching ramifications.

GLORIA: Remember we had a party at your place with all the men too. And then they formed a CR group. But they only met a few times. I often wonder if that may have changed them . . . may have given them some ideas.

RITA: Yeah, who was actually in that?

HELEN: I think everybody but Rose and Sophia had a husband in that group. My husband mentioned to me afterwards that the talk seemed to have got on to sexual hangups. And he didn't want to talk about that, but it made him wonder what we were talking about in the women's group. That's the first time he made that sort of comment to me.

RITA: I remember my husband telling me that the men's group was very important to him.

AGNES: I don't think mine kept going.

HELEN: No, mine didn't either. The only reason I remember the whole thing so well is because Bernadette's husband wrote a letter saying the group didn't give him what he wanted and he wouldn't continue with it. And I felt that as a personal insult for myself. Don't ask me why! I hadn't yet acquired the art of saying that's not my problem. And that made it difficult for me to communicate with Bernadette for a while. But then I had her over for lunch one day, and I said: 'Look, this is silly . . .' So we talked about the letter and everything was okay. Her husband was just very different from the other men, he was a hippie to me. And Rita's husband was much more modern too, more . . . alternative. We saw him looking after children, doing housework and cooking. But Agnes and I were married to very conservative men.

GLORIA: Of course, there was another reason why their group didn't last. There was a difference. We formed a group because we wanted to raise our consciousness. They formed a group because they were the husbands of the women.

AGNES: It was like the ladies' auxiliary in reverse.

The CR group was different from anything the women had ever been involved with. In the following conversation they share their early impressions of consciousness-raising and their relief at finding people with whom they could communicate and identify.

GLORIA: It was such a revelation. It was just so wonderful that there were women there who seemed to be on my wavelength and weren't putting me down . . .

RITA: . . . who didn't expect that if I couldn't run up a dress in half an hour . . .

GLORIA: Yes! And see, I've been sort of listening and thinking. I came from a family of six girls, and my parents were migrants. And they were terrified that their daughters wouldn't get married. So all we were told to do was grow up as soon as possible . . . seventeen, eighteen . . . and find ourselves a Jewish husband. It didn't matter if he had two heads and no education . . . but he had to be Jewish.

Now when I married my first husband, my parents didn't even look at his family, who were quite mad . . . around the bend! But instead of saying well, the family's not too good and he doesn't look too good either, they thought, *We'll get her married and then she's off our hands.*

I was taught to not make any waves . . . to do the right thing. And I really resent my parents for that. I always wanted to be a teacher. Always. But I wasn't even game to mention it because my oldest sister ended up teaching, and the trouble, and the arguments that went on . . . Mum always said that out of all the daughters she had I was the quietest, the most malleable. And I realised that I did everything to please them.

It didn't seem to worry them that their daughter had married this man who was hopeless. He used to belt me. I had to take him to court a couple of times. He tried to run over me in the car. And my father sat in the court and heard it all, and said: 'You should go back home. Your place is with your husband. And it's your fault; it's something you're doing'. And I was also told not to make waves because I had a younger sister who still had to get married and if I disgraced the family nobody would marry her. And it went on and on.

In those days there was nothing I could do. I had only learned basic office skills so I could support myself until I got married, but what was that? I'd forgotten whatever shorthand I had. I couldn't get a proper job to support myself and the two kids.

I was just completely trapped. And I read somewhere that lots of these battered wives turn to their families and they get told it must be something they're doing. Or to go home because Christmas is coming and they should have a nice holiday with the family and make everything seem nice.

RITA: It's the old story. She gets what she deserves. Even if it's rape or murder.

GLORIA: Yes. Dad said: 'You must have shouted at him'.

RITA: A few years ago, the prevailing attitude was that it was the woman's fault. But just recently, in the last three or four weeks, it has begun to come into the public view. On two Australian shows — 'A Country Practice' and 'E Street' — there's been a battered wife who has said: 'Oh, it must be my fault. I must be doing something'. And there's been another person . . . a doctor or a lawyer or someone . . . who's said: 'No, it isn't you. He's the one with the problem'. You know, coming out and saying it.

HELEN: Yes, of course now you can get him for assault. The law has changed now.

AGNES: Well, I know it's important that the laws change. But still, I've seen interviews with habitual wife-beaters . . . and I don't think laws make any difference to them. I remember one who was in jail . . . in some group therapy session, and he had tears rolling down his face . . . and then he started talking about it . . . what used to be happening when he beat her up. And even though part of him felt really bad about what he'd done, you know what he said?

'But she wouldn't shut up!' And that's the bottom line. What he's saying is that there's nothing else you need to know . . . she wouldn't shut up! After the laws have been changed and after everything that had happened to him . . . still, this seemed like a good reason for belting her. You could tell that underneath the layers of remorse, and even of self-pity . . . underneath that you could almost see him getting mad again just thinking about it. In fact if he had her there then he'd have given her another whack. So, I just can't trust these men.

GLORIA: Well, I know my first husband is still in therapy because of these problems. And the problems go back to his own childhood. He had terrible parents.

RITA: Yes, but why should you suffer because of his childhood!

GLORIA: I know, but I had no support . . . in those days women's refuges didn't exist, or they were just starting. If there was a deserted wife's pension I didn't know about it. I didn't know any of my rights. Who did in those days? So I was caught in that trap. It wasn't till I joined the group that I started to see other possibilities.

RITA: Oh, I found the group exciting! You asked me before what I expected to be when I was a child. Up to the age of fourteen I guess I had a certain idea about myself and what I might become. But then when I was fourteen I had an accident which changed my life entirely. I was in the hospital for a long time . . . and then three years later I got married. And then not too long after that I had the boys.

I guess if I hadn't had the accident I wouldn't have got married until I was a fair bit older. But then, I sort of figured I needed protection. Oh, I'd been out in the work-force for a couple of years before I got married, but there was always Mother. And she would protect me to a certain extent. But I knew that I couldn't expect to be protected by her all my life. I realised that she had her own life that she needed to live, and so I thought, oh well, I'll get married.

So I didn't really have a chance to work out an identity for myself before I got married. And so, becoming involved in the women's group was more a part of my search for self-discovery.

AGNES: I don't remember thinking about growing up. I just kind of expected things to go on forever the way they were. I didn't think about the future. In fact, when I realised one day that I was actually *in* my future . . . that the present was it . . . I thought, god, I'm not prepared for this. I don't know what I want to be or do.

I met my husband when I was still in high school. Along with that femininity thing went not being practical at all . . . you had to be not very good at looking after yourself. And I wasn't. So I found somebody who was happy with the role of protector. I was a bit of an airhead.

I eased into the group. There wasn't an initial 'Oh, wow, I'm glad I'm here!' I didn't feel that it was what I'd been waiting for all my life. I was a little suspicious because I had never thought of other people as being like me, so I didn't quite know what to make of the group. And in fact, in many ways they weren't like me. But that was actually okay. It took me a while to figure out that the idea wasn't to find a group where everybody was alike, but one where it was okay to be different.

I didn't have many friends of my own. I only had the wives of husband's friends, or neighbours. A lot of my self-esteem came from this really strong sense of being feminine in a traditional way. I totally identified with that whole thing . . . not so much being submissive, but . . . pretty, soft . . . And I still had a lot of prejudices that the general public had I think. Like the bra-burning story.

The really hard thing for me was telling the truth about myself. I wasn't used to it. I think I had to get to the truth a layer at a time, and there were a few layers. I think the biggest thing the CR group did for me was to get me to stop rewriting my life story. I lied so much, I even lied to myself. I made up this story about my virginity because men didn't like you if you weren't a virgin. And I told the story so many times that in the end I couldn't remember when I lost it. My husband probably didn't give a damn. But at the time, I believed a woman had to protect herself. That was one of the things you learned along with cooking, cleaning, dressmaking, mothering . . . you learned to lie. That was a basic survival skill for women. And only a fool didn't know that. A woman would lie about her age, her weight, her sexuality . . . a woman would lie about anything, because she totally depended on the good will of others.

HELEN: Well, I arrived in that group and I thought, *Here are all my soul mates*. You see, all these issues that concerned Agnes I'd sorted out already. What I wanted was someone to talk with about feminism. I'd tried talking to the women in my neighbourhood, and they couldn't understand. They thought I was silly and they didn't want to get into that type of discussion. So when I found the group I thought, *Finally, I've arrived*. I can't tell you what it was like. I felt secure. Straight away I knew this was going to be it. People listened to me and they didn't brush aside what I was saying.

Then when the group finished it was okay because I'd had my say; I'd told people how I felt. I really . . . I enjoyed it. And I still feel the same with you all. I feel the same with other women who were part of the women's movement . . . it affects you. You can never go back. I have never been too extreme but I couldn't go back to before the whole group was formed. I still feel that thing when I'm with women.

AGNES: I do now. But, see, I grew up . . . without ever having a best girlfriend. Instead I had a series of best friends. You had one until she knifed you in the back — always something to do with a man — and then you went and got another one. In high school you could trust another girl with everything except your secrets, which always had to do with sex and boys, and you could not trust another girl to choose her friendship with you over a possible boyfriend. That was just accepted. You didn't forego the pleasure of a relationship with a fellow because he was somebody else's fellow. All was fair in love and war. How do you think it got to be a cliché?

So I certainly didn't think of women as allies. I thought of them from the very beginning as people who, no matter how close you got, you had to be careful about sharing confidences with because they could use them against you later. And you knew that if a man came on the scene there was a chance there'd be a fight over him. And that was like 'The Law'. I don't even know whether I liked it or approved of it. It was just a fact of life.

What was funny was that the only possible outcome you considered was that one woman would get the man. You never thought about two women saying: 'Let's go off together and leave him alone completely'. It's funny because now that does present itself as an alternative. That friendship could be the stronger desire.

HELEN: I never felt the way you did. But then we have different personalities, and different backgrounds. I always had a woman friend. And no man could have interfered with that. I'm still in contact with those women. We write great long letters. I think it's also the upbringing . . . I don't know . . . my mother always said to me: 'You make sure you have women friends because they are the only ones that will really stick to you'.

AGNES: My mother said exactly the opposite!

GLORIA: Actually, I think my mother's advice was like what Agnes got from her mother. I was taught to be devious. My mother certainly never told me to stick with other women.

HELEN: Isn't it funny. My mother also said to me . . . when I was getting married and leaving home for good . . . when I was leaning out of the window of the train, she said: 'Helen, there's some money in your name. I'll fix it up in the bank in your name because you have to have money. Make sure you have money of your own, and girlfriends, because you never know about men'.

AGNES: Well, my mother said always have a little money put aside. But that was more of the same philosophy: In your best interests, don't tell anyone everything. Once you're married you let him look after you, but you always have a little mad money that he doesn't know anything about. I'm only seeing this in retrospect. I never thought that my mother taught me to lie.

HELEN: If your mother heard you now, she would probably say that wasn't how she meant the whole thing.

AGNES: This isn't against my mother . . . it's just that when I look back I get a hell of a shock. I never thought of myself as a dishonest person because when we were asked to express opinions I was very upfront. But the fact is, there were certain foundations that I believed you were supposed to lay, and they were always laid in big lies!

HELEN: When you look at many of the magazines of the '50s and '60s, with those articles about how to behave as a woman . . . it was all a big lie, wasn't it. It was pretending. How you had to present yourself. And this was just a normal thing. I think perhaps I was just lucky . . . when I was a teenager we were talking about Dostoyevsky and Sartre. Catching the male wasn't so important.

AGNES: Yes, I always saw you as different. And I used to envy you so much. I was glad that there was somebody like you in the group. I can remember you telling us about your mother making sure that you had some contraceptives when you were a teenager and you were going overseas. You could have knocked me off my chair! I couldn't believe that your mother knew you were having sex . . . that she helped you . . . that you were telling us that you were having sex when you were that age . . . I just couldn't believe any of that stuff.

HELEN: Well, I still can't get over you saying that about the truth. I don't know, perhaps it's my personality. I just tell people the truth.

Of course sometimes I feel people don't like me because I am too truthful. But to me, in a group like that, it was essential that you were truthful right from the beginning. I just assumed that we were all telling the truth.

AGNES: Yes, and I just assumed that we were all lying.

HELEN: Well, what I did feel was that the group was the first place I could tell the truth and know I wasn't being judged.

AGNES: The group was a tremendous relief to me because . . . you see, when I talk about lying, mostly I'm referring to sex. But also, in the area of mothering, I could have cried with relief the first time somebody . . . Sue, I think . . . said she never read stories to her kids. Up till then I'd always felt I was surrounded by supermothers.

HELEN: See, you don't question. You see all these supermothers but that's often a pretense. Did you have to work hard at being a mother or did it come naturally?

RITA: Oh, I don't know if I ever worked hard at it. I always hoped . . . and maybe I assumed . . . that I was doing the right thing. When I was a child my mother was often very panicky about things . . . very nervy . . . and she put her panic into me. So I said to myself I would never be like that. I would always try to be cool and calm. So as long as I was cool and calm I figured I was doing the right thing.

But I'm interested in what Agnes was saying before, about assuming that we were all lying. What did you actually mean?

AGNES: I meant that I assumed each of you was protecting yourself just like I was . . . 'lying' is a very loaded word. I meant I couldn't imagine anyone leaving themselves totally vulnerable with the absolute truth about their history, and their thoughts. I wouldn't have expected it.

RITA: I remember when people would ask me questions about

myself and my life I would find it difficult to explain . . . not difficult to tell the truth, but to say the words that would convince me that I was making sense. Do you know what I mean?

AGNES: Well, I wasn't used to being asked questions that required me to look into myself for answers. So in the group I used to go on for a long time and not say very much.

RITA: Yes, that's what I mean.

AGNES: Often I didn't know what I was going to say until I heard myself say it. Nowadays I try to think about the answer first, but then I guess I was so delighted that people were asking me what I thought . . . and I was afraid that if I didn't say something straight away I'd lose my chance.

RITA: Yes, I would feel that if I didn't say what I wanted to say immediately I'd miss my chance. I don't think I thought much about what I was going to say. Afterwards, I would think about what I'd said. *(Rita gives a small self-deprecating laugh.)*

HELEN: What I learned in the group — and this was useful later on with my husband — was to verbalise what I felt. The whole thing was very beneficial. It was a process that took years, but it started with the group. I could say what I wanted to and it didn't have to be kept in my subconscious.

AGNES: Did you have victim dreams?

HELEN: Yes . . . big mountains trying to fall on me . . . or being pulled into the big emptiness of a swamp. Things like that. And I remember . . . I kept a diary when the group was going . . . I wrote down that the dreams were getting less and less frequent, and I wondered if it had something to do with me finally being able to talk to somebody.

AGNES: Also, when your image of yourself changes it must have an effect. I used to have lots of abandonment dreams . . . somebody was always leaving me . . . I don't think you can have dreams like that unless you've turned the responsibility for your well-being over to somebody else. I mean, I'm not abandonable nowadays.

RITA: As far as self-images go, I think mine was that I was pretty much a bad, evil person; that I did bad, evil things. And then in the group, when I started saying the things that I did I was never really quite convinced that it was acceptable to everybody. Sexual things mostly. But I kept on saying them because I didn't want to tell lies. I wanted to tell the truth as far as I could see it. And I think a few people were a little surprised, but nobody ever expressed disapproval or anything. At least not to me.

GLORIA: Oh, I think that was one of the good things. What was said there was accepted at face value, and there wasn't much judging. We were there telling each other all the things we couldn't tell anybody else, and I think we were all in the same boat, so we just accepted each other.

In discussing the dynamics of the old consciousness-raising group we had opened up a Pandora's box. The women were obliged to delve into a period of their lives which had been highly charged, and to focus on selves which they all felt they'd left behind. The hazards of asking people to wander down memory lane suddenly became obvious. Perhaps naively we hadn't anticipated that some old grievances and misunderstandings would need to be aired before the interviews could continue. Sometimes this was painful, but it was nothing the women hadn't done before.

The discussion ended with some comments about how the group had functioned and the particular ways in which it had been important to these members.

AGNES: Listen, that group belonged to us. Each one of us had an equal investment in it. We could do with it what we wanted; we could claim it for our own. We all had a right to talk about what mattered to us and if another person didn't like it she could say so.

HELEN: Yes, I always felt that we were free to say if we didn't like something.

GLORIA: But to a certain extent we were courteous. We were polite. Though I remember once when you *(to Helen)* did something really negative. You said to me I really should go to a mothers' club and bake some cakes and not come to a CR group. And I thought, *My CR group is saving my life and she wants me to go bake cakes!* That's what I was trying to get away from. But I was almost leading two lives . . . part of me was doing the mothers' club thing and making all the right noises . . . and I can see that if I said that in the group it might have given you the shits. But see, I was trying to please people out there, and to find my identity in here . . . and I thought . . . *How can she not understand?*

HELEN: But you see, that was the whole point about the group. There was such a dynamic. We were all from different backgrounds, different personalities . . . and I had negative feelings about others . . . sometimes about all of you. But I'm not afraid of negative feelings.

GLORIA: In a relationship with people where you're being very honest there must be times . . . you can't always think they're wonderful . . . there must be things that irritate you. Sometimes you see something in them that you see in yourself.

AGNES: Well, all that stuff made that group unique in my experience. Outside of it people just didn't talk that way to each other.

GLORIA: So, did it change your life for the better or the worse?

RITA: I want to say something in preface to that. My women friends had always been strong women . . . really strong . . . who would speak out if they felt like it. I never had women friends who were wimpy, stay-at-home, not-do-anything people. My best friend is someone who has done so much with her life against great odds.

But I didn't know many other women who were like that . . . hardly any. So when I came into the women's group it expanded this idea I had of the type of women I could associate with. It expanded greatly. And after I left, I guess that expansion, and the new horizons, were what I left with. New possibilities. Like . . . a flowering.

HELEN: I see that too. It gave me the impetus to do something I had always wanted to do — to go to university. To enlighten myself, and I think to actually find out what I wanted from life. I think it gave me the confidence. Yes, it expanded me.

GLORIA: Well, for me it was learning to trust other women, and realising just how emotionally supportive they could be. And then again, that gave me the confidence to do what I wanted to with my life as a woman.

HELEN: It was sort of a springboard. The wish was always there in my mind . . . I would like to go back to education, to do something with my life. But it wasn't clear. The group gave me the confidence. And all of us, I think. Look how many of us went back to school. I needed that support. Not somebody saying, 'Oh, that's nice', just to keep me quiet. Real support. And always, for what I have today, I'm so grateful to the group.

GLORIA: I know what it did. It gave me faith in myself. When so many people were still trying to pull me down, I thought, *Now, I can do it*.

RITA: I tell you what . . . I really could have used our weekly meetings . . . the group . . . in 1979, 1980. Why weren't you there?

HELEN: Well, the phone was there. No, actually we should have made some provision for having a recall if we all felt like it. Or if a few did. But then perhaps after three years we just felt we had to go out on our own.

The old days

AGNES: It suddenly strikes me as terribly sad that after all this great bonding which we spent several years creating, some of us went through the worst period of our lives without a great deal of support from other women at all. I'm not just talking about the group. I feel very strongly that I was quite alone except for spasmodic hits of friendliness from people. And I didn't ask. That's what's bad . . . I didn't ask.

HELEN: Yes, well, like I said, we all had each other's numbers.

AGNES: Yes. So what does it say about the trust that I was so sure I'd left with, if in fact I didn't trust people with my grief, or my confusion.

HELEN: You did, actually. Remember when I came to visit you when you were really and truly desperate. You did phone. But still . . .

AGNES: Yes, at certain critical times . . . well, you were very good to me. I guess I'm thinking more of the day-to-day thing of having a friend in my life, so that maybe instead of . . . having to be picked up and put together again . . . I wouldn't have broken in the first place. What if, through some kind of everyday ongoing contact, some of those horrible things were kept from happening . . . I never did establish that 'best friend' situation.

RITA: This is very interesting. Where was the group? Were we all a bit scared to get back, and not wanting to . . . I don't know . . .

AGNES: Well, this may sound like a contradiction, but I'm not sure I thought of the group as my new friends. I think the group served it's purpose. In those days people went to all sorts of groups. (*Laughs.*) If I went to a particular group it was for a particular reason. I wasn't actually looking to broaden my social circle. Ours was a functional group. And it was a very intimate group. But in a sense, to me it was only really valid in the long run if it wasn't just those few women I could work with . . . if I took what I learned inside the group out into the world.

So when I talk about going through things alone, I don't so much mean why didn't I get back in touch with the group. I mean why didn't my time in the group enable me to establish a sort of daily support system. Not something that came and bailed me out in a crisis, but something that maybe kept me from getting to crisis point. Why didn't my life change a bit more? *(Here everyone laughs, but there is an awkwardness about the laughter, as though the women recognise the truth of what Agnes is saying.)* We're talking about the group's impact, aren't we? If we look at how things changed, I guess we also have to look at how things didn't change.

GLORIA: Well, we all went on to do other things in our lives. I don't know how we're going to trace all changes exactly back to the group.

RITA: We're not just talking about the group. We're looking at the women's movement in general. Was there a revolution or just a storm in a teacup?

GLORIA: The group was the nucleus.

HELEN: It was the obvious place to start. The group had an identity . . . it was the group that gave us the confidence and the faith in ourselves, and taught us how to communicate with other women.

RITA: About things other than what I'd expected to talk to women about.

HELEN: And even just a simple thing like looking at the newspaper . . . the sexism in the media . . . there may have been awareness before, and a sense of injustice . . . but not as strong. And even now I notice those things. Well, it was a consciousness-raising group, wasn't it. It was consciousness on an individual level and a macro level . . . in society. Being aware of things like pay and promotions and the education of girls. I'm now very aware of the differences. I was never innocent . . . and the group in a way spoiled any chance I might have had of being innocent. I'm more critical.

AGNES: And my world view also changed, because through the women's movement for the first time I was exposed to women of different backgrounds, different classes, different ages.

HELEN: There was a big range when you went to the Women's Centre. And I still remember my very first one of those Saturday meetings. There was an architect and a lawyer and they were just like me. I thought I could never get to that level, but here they were, just speaking normally, and I thought, *Hey, I can do that too.* I think that was very important for me.

You know, in my generation intellectual women were something exceptional. I always half thought of them as goddesses . . . you know . . . and they weren't. The first time I realised they were just like me I knew that I was going to do something . . . going to arrive there. It just might take me a bit longer. That had a big impact on me.

RITA: It was important for me too that I had role models, women I could look up to but also talk to like ordinary people. When I was doing my Dip.Ed. in 1979 one of my tutors — she was several years older than me — actually invited me to come with her up to Sydney University, to attend a political economy conference. And I went and met some people . . . and it was great.

AGNES: The group had a big impact on me sexually. When I was growing up women pretended they didn't like sex. Then suddenly we were in an era when I felt as if I should pretend to like it more than I actually did. I mean, everybody was having orgasms all over the place, except me.

We did seem to spend a lot of time talking about sex. I remember my first orgasm. Bernadette had asked me if I ever masturbated and I said I didn't know how. What was I then . . . twenty-seven, twenty-eight? And I didn't know how. So she loaned me a book . . . I figured it out . . . and I had an orgasm. I'd been married eight years. So I don't associate orgasms with men, I associate them with *myself*. That was really revolutionary for me. *(Throughout Agnes's account of her sex education the women were in hysterics.)*

AGNES: Well, those were the days of *Cleo* and *Cosmopolitan* and articles about 'The Big O'. Suddenly women were rebelling against the idea of being the demure little lady who didn't really like sex but would go along with it for the sake of her husband's conjugal rights. So lots of women were coming out and saying: 'Stuff that, I've always enjoyed sex'. And here's me thinking . . . *Yeah, well . . . I'm not so sure.*

GLORIA: Yes, I can remember when that happened. You were quite happy about the whole thing.

AGNES: Well, those were the days of *Cleo* and *Cosmopolitan* and articles about 'The Big O'. Suddenly women were rebelling against the idea of being the demure little lady who didn't really like sex but would go along with it for the sake of her husband's conjugal rights. So lots of women were coming out and saying: 'Stuff that, I've always enjoyed sex'. And here's me thinking . . . *Yeah, well . . . I'm not so sure.*

When I was a teenager and it wasn't allowed I liked what I was able to get away with, but I was used to feeling guilty, and trying to keep myself under control. Then when I got married I couldn't seem to get *out* of control any more.

HELEN: That reminds me. I was about seventeen . . . it was about the second boyfriend I'd had, and I knew what I liked, you know . . . because the first boyfriend had been very good and he taught me a lot. He was only my age, but gee, he knew some things. And then the second one, he was a big beautiful hunk. Oh, he was the world. But when we had sex for the first time I didn't feel anything, because it was . . . in, out, in, out . . . and that's all. And then after a while I thought, *I don't like this. I like to be touched . . . I like to be kissed . . . I like this and that . . .* And being my honest self I said: 'I like that . . . you've got to touch me here . . . look, that's how you do it'. And you know what the idiot said to me? He said: 'That's not normal!' Well, I soon finished with him. But you know, I still dream about having my revenge, and if I ever saw him the first thing I'd say is: 'Hey, you didn't know how to make love. It wasn't my fault'. I had quite a hard time getting over that. *(Here the whole group laughs at the thought that these revelations will some day be read by other people.)*

AGNES: I had a similar experience to Helen's. It was about touching instead of being touched. I was sixteen and in the heat of the moment I put my hand some place he thought I shouldn't, and he said: 'Only whores do that!' You were supposed to just come together like that *(claps)* and then come apart. And that really hung me up for ages.

GLORIA: You both must have wondered if you *were* normal when they said those things, but really it was their problem.

RITA: You know, the myth that women are somehow sexually inferior is still being perpetuated on mid-day television. I saw this doctor the other day and he was saying that women must have to work much harder at having orgasms . . . and some women never have them, blah, blah. And I thought, *Am I hearing this?* Maybe in 1950 or 1960 even. But now? Some people just want to turn back the clock.

AGNES: Well, I never learned one single thing about good sex from a man. I don't care what hot stuff they thought they were. I don't say I haven't enjoyed it, but I cannot say any man ever *taught* me anything.

HELEN: There must be lots of women like that around. They learn things in conversations, or in books, or in that exploring stage. I mean, I explored myself very early. I was ten and a half when I got my period, and I was plagued by my feelings quite early, so I very soon found out exactly what was nice for me. I often think back and I can remember having those terrible feelings down here . . . and I think that's when my mother . . . she soon found out . . . and she gave me this book because it explained everything very well.

AGNES: And talking with other women was just so important. In the group we gave each other information about things and we gave each other permission to talk, and to be the way we were. And we demystified things. You know, I couldn't believe that Bernadette said that word 'masturbation' for a start.

GLORIA: Yes, there were certain words you didn't use.

AGNES: Absolutely. And Bernadette was very instrumental in my . . . well she just gave me more information. My basic personality didn't change, but that's okay. Some of my ability to accept myself as I am is the result of information I got from the group.

Interview 2: 24 April 1989
Bernadette, Helen and Agnes

Bernadette's job requires her to work irregular hours, so it was difficult for her to find a time when she could be interviewed. She was the only group member who hadn't been able to make it to the reunion.

This evening we started talking with Bernadette on her own, but were later joined by Helen and Agnes who had particularly missed seeing her at that first get-together. Bernadette began by explaining the circumstances surrounding her initial contact with the women's movement.

BERNADETTE: I got interested in the whole women's liberation thing through my concern about sexism in children's books, about role models that girls had. I had seen some feminists on television talking about it, and I was quite interested in the issue so I wrote to my local newspaper. It took me ages to actually make contact with the women's movement, and when I did they referred me to the closest CR group. It was quite a roundabout process.

The funny thing is that I was looking at women's liberation from a traditional point of view, wanting to be a good mother if I ever had female children. And I had a husband who supported my interest. What I didn't know at the time was that he had an ulterior motive. He wanted to get me involved in a movement that encouraged me to go out to work, so I could support *him* while he did his own thing. *(Bernadette gives an ironic chuckle.)*

Of course that changed when I really got angry. I went through a stage where I started to see men as the cause of women's problems — you know, male domination — and then he didn't like it so much.

This led to a discussion of the feminist backlash of the past decade. There was a time, in the '70s and '80s, when feminism was almost respectable. You could assume that if a woman was reasonably intelligent and socially aware she was to some extent sympathetic to feminism. Today it seems to have negative connotations for a lot of people.

BERNADETTE: And yet, like with other movements . . . like the hippies . . . certain things have been taken from it and absorbed into the culture, and used against us. Out of the women's movement they took the concept that women have to work. You could question whether this is the same thing as independence. When you look now at what's happened since that time . . . women have lost the option of staying at home. That wouldn't be so bad by itself, but you have a double role. You have to work at home and outside too. You haven't got an option, and part of what we were in the women's movement for was more options. Women are still responsible for most of the housework and childcare, so there's a lot more stress . . . but, in a way, women are smart not to lose that role, because when all's said and done, human relationships are a very, very important part of life, and if we lose that connectedness with life, we've really been conned, I reckon. Often we talk about the way men control things, and I think we're becoming more like that, and we've lost something in the process.

Here Bernadette recalls the days when Winsome McCaughey, then a principal member of the Women's Electoral Lobby, returned to Melbourne from New York after having done a lot of work there in the area of childcare. A great deal of energy went into planning strategies for childcare in Australia.

Unfortunately, to this day no satisfactory childcare program exists. Though the facilities have expanded since the 1970s, when there were only 25 centres in Victoria, they are extremely expensive. Women who work outside the home have to pay as much as a quarter of their weekly income to have their children looked after.

And now, in the name of equal opportunity, women have the same retirement age as men, but it's not about equality. It suits the government to save that five years' worth of pension payment for women. Everything gets used to sort of foster another end altogether, other people's selfish interests . . . whether it's the government or my ex-husband. So in the end, I feel a bit cheated by the movement.

(Here Bernadette returns to the subject of motherhood.)

In that book of Betty Friedan's, *The Feminine Mystique*, she talks about how we repeat patterns we learned from our mothers. But I felt that when you looked at what it took to be a good mother you discovered that you had to be a person first. If you believe that, it turns things around. You no longer focus on being a good mother but you come face to face with who you are and what you're doing in your life. And that is what you offer as a parent — the person you are. That certainly wasn't what I'd learned from *my* mother.

When you're young and you have this fantasy about growing up and getting married, you don't see yourself as developing beyond that point. You see yourself as static. As a teenager, when I'd pictured my future, I was always married with two children. There was nothing else. And the reality is different. It's all been a rude shock.

That sounds awful but it's true. I thought I could assume this role, and that I would never have to go through that process of taking responsibility for myself and my life. Actually it was very childlike. *(Laughs.)* I don't think I'll ever get over it. I think I'll be coming to terms with it for the rest of my life.

As a child I was never listened to, or allowed to be an individual. It was 'Be seen and not heard'. Don't think, don't say what you think, don't ask questions. Really, I was almost invisible. There was no process of discovering where the boundaries of who I was came into contact with other people's boundaries. Ideally you allow your children to express themselves, and then explore that somehow. But there was none of that in my parents' home. Children just fitted in. Nobody thought of them as people. What I picked up was to not be a person.

But I was very afraid too, because my sister fought it, and she was very badly punished as a result. My father believed that you train children like you do puppies . . . break their spirit . . . show them who's the boss. So I just decided to not express myself, not wanting to go through what she had. She was rebellious, but it didn't do her any good. Well, maybe it did, it's hard to say.

At this point the interview was interrupted by the arrival of Agnes and Helen who were keen to catch up with Bernadette. During a break for coffee the issue of contraception was raised, and the revolution which the Pill and abortion on demand created in the lives of women of their generation. Agnes had recently been to a reading of the play 'Angels of Power' *by Sandra Shotlander, in which a pregnant woman finds out that her husband, who is a doctor, has implanted in her some eggs from his dead mistress. By the time the interview resumed, the three women were deep into a discussion about reproductive technology.*

AGNES: I think there's always a danger of women being objectified and manipulated when they're looked at as reproducers. Whether it's our desire for motherhood, or for abortions, or our willingness to be incubators. What about the women who can't be mothers, or don't want to? I wish we didn't define ourselves by that role.

HELEN: But my concern is that eventually that role will be taken over by a test tube, a reproduction machine.

BERNADETTE: I wonder about that too. Birth and nurture, it's the mystery of life, isn't it? It's a miracle. And I think men have always been a bit jealous. You can talk about penis envy and that, but there is a primitive element in the way women are joined to nature and male creativity has always been a bit hollow in comparison. Men have had to give birth to something of their own in a more abstract way . . . through their work, or art . . . And now they start playing with test tubes, and trying to create life.

HELEN: I think this is important. This is the last thing that makes us women and it's being taken over by men.

BERNADETTE: It's sort of crazy, isn't it. Equality is being taken very literally. It's sort of a non-acceptance of the differences between males and females.

Eventually the conversation returned to Bernadette's experience of the CR group. She admits that one of her strongest impressions from those days revolves around her shock at finding out that several of the women were having extra-marital affairs.

BERNADETTE: I was always a goodie-goodie. I always took things very seriously . . . religion and that. I always tried to do what you were supposed to do. And to hear all these people who had so many lovers. I'm thinking of one in particular, who enjoyed herself so much. *(The women all laugh remembering tales of exploits.)* And she used to tell us all the different things she did and I could not believe that people really did these things. I guess that I must not have approved, really. I always thought you had to be totally honest with your partner; that if you were going to have affairs you'd have to be out in the open about it. I was quite gullible. It was a big shock to discover what other people's sexuality was really like.

AGNES: Were you surprised that they didn't seem to feel guilty? That was the part that surprised me.

BERNADETTE: Oh, yes. They were just having so much fun. And to me there were very serious implications in that. It was not only the doing it, but the dishonesty as well.

AGNES: I can remember you and your husband talking about how you believed in total honesty, in everybody telling everybody everything.

BERNADETTE: Well, I took that really seriously. But he had ulterior motives. Even after we separated he could keep tabs on me. And he could tell me all about how his new girlfriend had multiple orgasms.

He gave me a book about orgasms. Something must have happened to me as a child . . . not to masturbate, to be so scared to touch myself . . . I don't know what it was, I don't have any memory of it. I didn't even know I had a clitoris till I was nineteen.

HELEN: Oh, stop! I don't believe it.

AGNES: No, I told you, it was the same for me. In fact, Bernadette loaned me that book* her husband gave her! And, don't you remember, Bernadette, you asked me if I ever masturbated and I told you I'd tried once, but I didn't realise there was any particular spot I was supposed to be aiming for so it didn't do much for me. I was so stupid. It was when I was about fifteen and I was sitting in the bathtub, and I thought, *Well, if this is all there is to it, I don't know what the fuss is about.* I was twenty-six or twenty-seven before I found out different.

(At this point the laughter, which has been threatening to erupt while Agnes and Bernadette have been speaking, suddenly becomes uncontrollable.)

BERNADETTE: You know, it's not a laughing matter, though I think you have to laugh about it now . . .

HELEN: No, you're right.

AGNES: But the two of us did sort of miss out somewhere along the line, because even my mother . . . I told her when I finally had an orgasm and she said: 'You've been married eight years. I don't know

---

* Belliveau and Richter, *Understanding Human Sexual Inadequacy*, Coronet, London, 1973.

how you stood it!' And I was quite shocked that my mother took orgasms for granted.

BERNADETTE: Remember the books about sex and contraception. A lot of those were initiated by the women's movement. A lot of information about things like that, and about abortion and fertility clinics. Things have changed a lot, haven't they, as a result of that period.

AGNES: Absolutely. And you know, when we had our first interviews, and we were talking about what stood out in our minds about those days, I said 'SEX'. Not the doing of it, but all those other things . . .

BERNADETTE: We never had a chance to *talk* about it before.

AGNES: No, and it wasn't trivial. It was absolutely mind-blowing that I didn't know my own self . . .

BERNADETTE: . . . your own body. There were lots of women who had no one else they could really open up to. You didn't have a sister, and I didn't talk to my sisters about those things because I didn't let them know what I was up to.

AGNES: The group was the only place I could satisfy my curiosity about everything. There was a whole other world of female experience that I knew nothing about, and women outside the group wouldn't discuss it. I don't just mean orgasms . . . I mean, just having fun with sex. I didn't feel disturbed about that like you did. I just found it very surprising. Because for me, sex and guilt went hand in hand. And another thing that surprised me was that it seemed to be the older women who were . . .

BERNADETTE: . . . less inhibited. Yes.

HELEN: Maybe it had something to do with maturity.

BERNADETTE: Oh, it was upbringing too. Certainly with you.

HELEN: Yes, and I did have other friends I could talk to, openly. But I felt lucky to get into a group.

At this point everybody had another good laugh. Then Bernadette considered what had been the most important thing the group had given her.

BERNADETTE: *(after a long pause)* I think it was something of my own . . . like personal exploration. You know those Monday nights . . . I remember once I was getting ready to go to a meeting and my husband said: 'Don't think I'm going to be enjoying myself while you're gone'. I had no compunction about going. That was his problem. It was my own thing, and I guess it was the first time I'd ever had anything of my own.

HELEN: Yes, I remember my husband having his birthday, and I went to a meeting. I just said to him: 'I'm sorry but I'm going' and I went. I'd never done it before and I haven't done it since, but during that period nothing could have kept me away. I lived for it, I was waiting for it.

As well as those weekly meetings, some of the women in the group had frequently visited the Women's Centre in the city.

BERNADETTE: Yes, I was on one of the collectives, and I did different things. And there were meetings with other women which were pretty good too.

HELEN: And remember, we supported the Centre financially, took collections, and some times we did some work there. I remember we went a few times to do some painting. Generally the women who went there were more radical than we were. I definitely wouldn't have worn lipstick there, and I was a bit worried about bringing a male child in there. There may actually have been a rule forbidding boys in the Centre.

This recollection led to others about divisions and prejudices which had existed within the women's movement, where there was sometimes considerable tension surrounding issues of race, class and the ideal of sisterhood. Rightly or wrongly, our CR group had always seen itself as being not really representative of the wider movement. *While most married middle-class women were to some extent affected by women's liberation, we actually identified ourselves with it, rather than with a more socially acceptable alternative such as the Women's Electoral Lobby.*

BERNADETTE: I remember sitting with you at the Centre, and they used to discriminate against housewives with children.

AGNES: It's interesting to hear you say that, because I only have my memories, and I wasn't sure if they were just sour grapes. I remember really having my feelings hurt because I wrote an article for *Vashti's Voice** about the differences in the way we treat little boys and little girls. For me, it was important. It represented so much soul-searching. Of course, it probably seemed very elementary to the editorial collective. They weren't interested in kids, much less in articles about them. So it didn't get printed. And I'd been told that they never left out anybody's contribution. But it mustn't have been radical enough. And that was when I realised that *we* were different. We had *real* decisions to make. Our *lives* were on the line. Nothing was abstract or hypothetical for us. Everything we decided to believe in . . . we were going to have to turn around and use . . . and live with the consequences. We didn't have clean slates. We had to do some erasing. We had to do some rewriting. And that's when I started feeling resentful of the women who I thought were judging me.

BERNADETTE: Yes, they had a real hide when you think of it. Of course, not everybody was like that. The ones that were genuine, like Bon Hull and Zelda,† those sort of people . . . they accepted all of us.

HELEN: To me, it seems feminism should include many ideologies.

BERNADETTE: Well, that was the beauty of it in the beginning.

---

* *Vashti's Voice* — Melbourne's women's liberation newspaper.
† Well-known Melbourne feminists of the '60s and '70s.

HELEN: Yes, but in the end I felt very much pushed into a corner.

BERNADETTE: I remember the way women dealt with all those barriers . . . different classes, different political views . . . That was partly why the women's movement started. But it became a little microcosm of what things were like on the outside. Not in our CR group, but in the larger movement.

There were separatists who would have nothing to do with other feminists. They had decided that their way, which was to exclude men, was the only way. I remember that when I started to see that happening in the movement . . . that was the end of it for me. I could no longer be involved.

AGNES: I think I only felt really comfortable in our CR group.

BERNADETTE: We could all be ourselves there, even if we were different from each other. Well, Sophia had a very different lifestyle from the rest of us at that time, but we didn't say she had to be like us and she didn't say we had to be like her.

AGNES: In fact, she chose to be in our group because she knew she would never come into contact with women like us unless she made an effort to.

HELEN: There was another problem for me. I like organisation in things. The meetings at the Centre attempted to get away from the kind of organisation which was seen as a male model. So there was nobody you could look at and say: 'That person is in charge'. I don't mean a leader, but even someone to just chair things, to give them a bit of order. It was supposed to be democratic, but I always felt that the most radical women had the floor all the time and we in the middle were often forgotten.

I got quite antagonistic. Also, it was assumed that you were automatically pro this political issue, and anti that one. There was a stereotype for how you would feel and act and think. *(Pause.)* Still, it was an era, and I'm very glad I went through it.

BERNADETTE: Yes, it was part of history being made. That's what someone said to me the other day. She'd been reading a book about that time, and she realised that we actually lived through all that.

HELEN: . . . and we're still living.

Bernadette returns to the subject of the group's impact on her ability to communicate with other women.

BERNADETTE: Getting to know each other with no men present . . . that was the big thing. We could just be women, no matter who our husbands thought we were. There was no pretending.

And I think one thing we all got was the knowledge that we're responsible for ourselves, no matter what. We all know that, don't we? Some people are better at handling responsibility than others though. *(She pauses for a moment.)* The group was great. Although I do remember at the time being disappointed that it wasn't more political. Because I thought we were going to change the world.

HELEN: Yes, and I guess we have changed it in our little way.

AGNES: Would you call yourself a feminist if someone asked you today?

BERNADETTE: No.

HELEN: *(to Agnes)* Would you? I would.

AGNES: Yes, but I'm aware that a lot of people wouldn't.

BERNADETTE: No. It's not a denial. It's more that I see myself as a person first, rather than a female. I don't see myself as an oppressed woman.

HELEN: Well, I would want to define what I meant by 'feminist' because of the connotations that feminism has today. This sometimes gets me into a lengthy explanation, but I don't care because every time I define it for someone else I do it for myself again.

BERNADETTE: Is the definition different today?

HELEN: That depends on who I'm talking to. Sometimes I leave things out because I think it's no use. If I know someone expects a deeper explanation I give them one. In a nutshell, I'd say feminism means believing in equality and choices.

AGNES: I sometimes wonder if I hang on to that label because I'm worried that a lot of people are letting go of it, and I still don't think that we've accomplished everything we set out to. It bewilders me when women who think the way I do about the issues won't call themselves feminists. It's not all I am, but I do believe in it.

HELEN: I think it's important that the word be still used, and be explained. I feel the way you do, and I like the word 'feminist'. I wouldn't want to deny it. I may have modified my ideas but I still believe in the principles.

BERNADETTE: I think I do too. I believe that choices should be available to women and that they should be equally rewarded for those choices. There are just some things that I don't choose to fight about. *(She pauses for a few moments.)* I think probably the reason we were all in the group was that we were looking for the best way to live our lives. We might not have always talked in a strictly philosophical way, but there was a sense of wanting to discover something. It was definitely a philosophical issue for me.

From the time I was a kid there was always a search for the best way to live. And it's been there in things I've done since. In anarchism. In my attempts to bring sexuality into the political realm, which was disastrous, really. *(Bernadette gives another of her frequent short laughs in which she seems to be saying 'The joke was on me').* There's been an attempt to do the right thing in a practical way; taking these philosophies and making them my own.

Also we were looking at the family structure: nuclear families, neighbourhood houses and communal living. They were all part of what was going on at the time. It was a real exploration of all the alternatives, and which ones were right for us.

Asked if she felt the group had given her anything which contributed to her life and career, Bernadette repeated that she felt she'd been conned, not by the group but by the women's movement which promised her some choices but took others away. She feels that the option to have a more traditional lifestyle has been denied her, emotionally as well as socially. Always completely honest, even when voicing unfashionable sentiments, Bernadette said: 'I can't live anymore in a situation where somebody else makes the choices for me, and yet I'm not really happy having to do everything for myself.'

HELEN: Are you saying, then, that the whole thing messed up your life?

BERNADETTE: No, No. I don't blame anything . . . it was sort of inevitable.

AGNES: It's like the slaves who were set free and had to deal with a whole new set of problems . . . like finding jobs and making decisions. Not that they wanted to go back to slavery, but the point is, they couldn't go back anyway.

BERNADETTE: Yes, and I don't feel I've made the transition successfully. I really feel that I would have liked a career as a home-maker, and to have fully enjoyed that. But the only way you can have a career as a home-maker is if some male supports you. And since being dependent is not satisfactory, you'd have to have the sort of relationship where you were recognised as an equal. And it's hard, even if you believe that's possible, to get the behaviour to fall into place, against all the old conditioning. So I've been forced to find work in the outside world, which isn't what I wanted.

But I did get a lot out of the group . . . being able to openly talk with other women about being a woman. So many different aspects of that were covered . . . all the things you're not allowed to talk about socially . . . There was this little place where it was okay to find out what other women were really like.

Interview 3: 9 May 1989
Sophia, Sue and Jane

It was some months before we were able to get Sophia, Sue and Jane together. Each of them came straight from work, and after a little dinner and a glass of wine to help them unwind, they were ready to reminisce, beginning at the beginning.

SOPHIA: Well, I remember that I was a very unhappy teenager. My parents wanted me to stay at home and be a nice young Italian girl. I wanted something different . . . I didn't quite know what but I thought maybe an education was a vehicle to getting it. At school I was quite miserable. I was very unsure about what I was going to do next. I read a lot of stuff about careers . . . not necessarily ones women could get into but ones for men . . . I just wanted to be somebody . . . I wanted to make something of myself. I didn't want to do what my parents did.

So in my first year at university I looked around to see what I could get involved in, particularly from a social point of view. I wanted to meet people who would present me with avenues for what I could do with my studies when I'd finished. And being Italian I joined the Italian Club. You see, I imagined that an Italian Club at university meant they all got together and talked about serious intellectual subjects.

I was shocked to find that really it was all about wine and cheese, and getting a ring on the finger from the guy who was studying Law or Engineering or Medicine. And then at the end of the first year, I suddenly found that a whole lot of women dropped out of the club. They'd found their bloke and there was no need to go on. And I thought, *Oh, no, this is not for me.*

So at the beginning of my second year . . . I was coming down the lifts at Monash and I saw these big posters announcing a Women's Liberation Club forming at the university. I'd vaguely noticed some stuff in the paper about these women in the United States who were burning their bras and I'd just thought it was . . . ridiculous! So I thought I'd go along for a joke . . . you know.

Now the first two meetings had a vehement debate about whether or not they'd allow men to stay in the meeting. There were all these really serious women, and I was just entertained by the power struggle. But in those discussions they talked about why they didn't want men there; about how men had dominated women's lives, and how we'd grown up being shaped into a particular role . . . to be feminine, etc . . . and men didn't share those same pressures.

Suddenly, as soon as I heard these women talk about this role stuff, the penny dropped! And I thought, *That's me!* All those years I've been unhappy because I didn't want to be the daughter at home, getting married, having babies, washing dishes . . . and suddenly it all made sense to me. It really talked to me . . . this discussion of sex role conditioning, and I just sort of became addicted to the truth. The more I went back, and the more I heard, the more it sounded true. So that's how I got involved. And then I became active on campus, and that led me to becoming involved with women organising off campus.

SUE: But how on earth did you get involved with *our* CR group? I mean, we were so different.

SOPHIA: You've got to remember, I was also a good Italian daughter. I had taken a room with some women in Carlton. Half the week I was living there and half the week I'd come out to the suburbs and stay with Mum. Obviously I didn't want her to know about the politics I was involved in, so I sort of lived a double life, going backwards and forwards from Carlton to the suburbs. The nights the CR group was meeting happened to be the nights I was at my mother's house. It was just geography . . .

But before that I was involved with another group. They were very political. No one revealed too much about their lives. Actually they used political discussions as a way of diverting from the true consciousness raising. And that's really what drew me to our group.

JANE: My memory is of being unhappily married. I'd seen advertisements for the Women's Electoral Lobby, but didn't feel confident about getting involved in that. Then I saw an advertisement about helping to get women elected to local politics . . . which was very unusual in those days . . . and I got on the committee. But I wasn't confident there either because they all seemed to be women who had jobs and qualifications.

Then I saw an article on women's liberation and a notice of a meeting at the Box Hill Town Hall. My daughter was just born . . . she was two months old . . . and I had to get a baby-sitter so I could go. There were heaps of people there. They took around a clipboard and you signed your names if you wanted to form a CR group. That was a really scary thing to do . . . to sign this when you didn't know what it would mean.

I don't know really what the catalyst was, except that I was unhappy with my lot, and I'd had that feeling since I was a kid. My father used to say to me: 'Be a good girl and iron your brothers' shirts'. I used to have to clean the bathroom and they didn't. So I knew back then that there was something wrong, but I accepted it . . . even though I didn't like it. When I went to the meeting at Box Hill, I certainly liked the sound of what they said, and I wanted to pursue it . . . but I was a bit scared.

Following that meeting at the Town Hall various suburban meetings were held with a view to establishing CR groups at a local level. Jane got Sue to go along with her to one of these, where they met Bernadette who was an organiser. Though this experience seems to have been a little intimidating, it didn't alter Jane's and Sue's determination to find a group to which they could belong.

SUE: Neither of us were really happy. I wouldn't have done anything about it, but Jane was far more motivated. We were home with young babies and no money. We didn't have jobs and we were reliant on the men coming home — hers never came home and mine was always at home.

And as Jane said it was scary . . . that first meeting we went to. I thought they all seemed too angry . . . there was no one I could really relate to. Bernadette really terrified me. She was so intense and serious, and I thought . . . perhaps this isn't for me. Perhaps I'm not deep enough. But I knew I was angry about a lot of things and miserable, and Jane was saying let's do something about this.

JANE: There were some very middle-class women at that meeting . . . and I went smelling like a chop because I'd rushed out of the house, so I was really self-conscious, which probably didn't help. You got the impression from this group that the movement was only for the educated middle class, except that I remember Bernadette was there. She was the one who told us which CR group was closest to us.

SUE: Were there many CR groups?

SOPHIA: Yes, there was a board at the Centre, and we had a map of the suburbs with little pins where there were groups, so when a woman rang we could look at the map and say: 'Your nearest group is such and such'.

SUE: I have *never* met anybody else who was in a CR group.

SOPHIA: Well, there were a lot more groups out the other side of town, and in the inner suburbs. And I can certainly remember when I used to tell my friends in the collectives that my CR group was in the eastern suburbs they'd all go, 'What are they like?' *(The women are amused by this confirmation of what they always suspected.)*

The Women's Liberation Newsletter, *March 1973, lists thirty-four consciousness-raising groups in the Melbourne area and one in Geelong. There was a group at each of the three universities and a concentration of groups in the Carlton-Fitzroy area. According to this list, there were only two western suburban groups servicing Maribyrnong and Glenroy-Essendon. The remainder were located in the eastern suburbs, spread out from Greensborough-Watsonia in the north to Aspendale in the south.*

It is worth remembering that until 1974 tertiary students paid fees. These details are interesting in the light of Jane's first impression that the groups were composed of 'educated middle-class' women. Obviously, Sophia's memory of 'groups out the other side of town' refers to the inner-city groups, many of which acted as satellites around Melbourne University.

SUE: Yeah, you were the only one in our group who wasn't married with children. And you didn't change your shoes before meetings like I did. Trying to get the image right. *(Sue gives an embarrassed laugh, and several of the other women join in, remembering their own attempts to fit the stereotype of a feminist activist.)*

SOPHIA: No, . . . no, I didn't do that, but I didn't change my group either.

SUE: And we loved you for it.

SOPHIA: When I think of all the pressures and comments — the disapproving comments . . . you know, people would say: 'Are they political out there, or what?' And I'd say, well, they're married and they've got kids and they're struggling with their lives, and they've all got issues to deal with. They haven't got time to be marching up and down the street. They're just trying . . . they throw in their money, and they're really interested in knowing what's happening.

JANE: So much for 'the personal is political'! I thought we *were* political in our own way.

SOPHIA: Well, you were. I never got drawn in by their attitude. Those women in the collective were either still students or they'd cut off from their husbands a long time ago, and they had very strong independent lives. Whereas you were still caught up with the battles and the decisions about which way to go. Personal development always came through as a major issue. And of course it was great, because it gave every confirmation for why I shouldn't get married.

SUE: Didn't you ever feel out of place with us, because you were so different?

SOPHIA: Occasionally I'd get frustrated because I'd think, *Why are they always going over the same things — don't they know the answer is just leave, pack up and go.* I'd met women who had made those decisions. I was young, you know, and the solution seemed quite simple. Now, coming back and hearing where everybody's at . . . well, it's just blown me away because you *did* make those decisions.

JANE: They might have been simple, but they certainly weren't easy.

SOPHIA: No, and everybody makes them in their own time.

SUE: I was glad you were in our group, because as long as you were, it could never turn into a knitting group. You know what I mean? But I used to think it might be boring for you. For instance, when we used to talk about sex, and we were all heterosexual.

SOPHIA: Yes, but all that stuff about what girls were supposed to be and do, as distinct from what boys could be and do . . . that was relevant for me too. And that whole description of courtship and sexuality . . . how men always sort of had the lead role. And then that stuff about rape. My first sexual encounters were with men . . . cringing in the back seat of the car. They'd always be in control and I'd have to fight them off. There was that horrible feeling of having no power and no control. They said I was an equal, but my feelings were not those of an equal, and when you're so young and impressionable it's confusing.

But also, most of my energy was going into other things. The group met during a period when I was more politically involved. I certainly wasn't highly sexual.

SUE: You were much more concerned with the world around you and I didn't even know about the world . . . I just wanted to get myself straight. The women's movement changed my entire life. I don't regret it, but it did . . . does . . . put me apart, because I made everyone else so angry, and I alienated myself from everyone.

JANE: I don't think I had an agenda when I got to the group, unless it was to get some reassurance that how I felt about being a female was okay. I'd come from a family of seven brothers where ironing shirts was seen as good for me, and I was married to a man who only saw a female as a servant . . . So I needed reassurance that I was okay. But I think once I actually got to a CR group, I didn't have that agenda anymore. I was just very happy to go along with what was happening. I just felt sort of cosy.

This led to a discussion on the various reactions of families and friends to the women's involvement in the movement.

SOPHIA: Well, I don't think there were any lovers, and I didn't really let my family in on what I was doing. But it had an important impact on a group of friends from my teenage years.

Sophia tells of her involvement with an Italian social club which held weekly dances where she and her friends would go to find boyfriends. She recalls her mounting anger at the male dominance that existed within these sorts of institutions, and her single-handed attempts to challenge what were entrenched cultural values.

And that's when I lost all my Italian friends . . . everyone who had belonged to my teenage years. I then realised I had to have *political* friends. I remember feeling like a leper. It changed the direction of my life because up till that point I still felt very strongly about my culture, and about staying Italian even though I was in Australia. But then I felt I had to let go of it because the Italian community was so awful and sexist, and there was no one in it who was politicised.

JANE: So that wonderful feeling you'd had when you went to the first women's meeting . . . of finally being in the right place . . . turned into a kind of disaster for you.

SOPHIA: Yes, I realised that I would be part of a very small group instead of a very large one.

JANE: I guess most of us never fully appreciated that cultural thing; how much harder it must have been for you coming from such a traditional society.

SOPHIA: I was doubly isolated. Not only because of my views, but I didn't have other Italians or Europeans in the movement that I could talk to and say: 'How are you dealing with all of this? What does *your* mother think? What about the whole Catholicism bit and the cross-cultural stuff?' I had no one else I could relate to about that, and that's where the movement let me down. It was very Anglo-Saxon orientated for many years. There wasn't any outreach to migrants. There has been lots in the last seven or eight years. But not in those first five.

JANE: Well, I had a terrible reaction from my family about my involvement with the movement. I was told that I was under the influence of my lesbian mates. When I was going to the WEL meetings, my husband used to say to the kids: 'Your mother's going out now, she doesn't want to be home with you children'.

The actual CR meetings were never an issue; going to them was just accepted until there were problems. And the closer I got to leaving home, the more problems there were. Then the group became an issue.

SUE: Yes. My husband resented me going to meetings.

SOPHIA: Was the group ever blamed for the breakups?

JANE: Actually, the meetings had finished by that time, but I knew the group was a very significant factor in our breakup. It made me stronger, more confident in deciding what I was going to do. If I hadn't gone to the meetings, I would still have got out, but it might have taken longer.

SUE: No, my marriage survived the group. I lasted another ten years after it disbanded.

At this point Sue explained that the group alone couldn't have given her the determination she needed to leave her bad marriage. She had been unhappy but ambivalent. She talked about a weakness in herself, and a certain stubbornness. This reflection on marriage led to a discussion about the insecurities felt by the partners of the CR group members when other members started separating. Sue said that after Jane separated her husband used to comment: 'I guess you'll be next'. Then both women talked about what it was like to be on their own after their marriages ended.

JANE: When Sue's marriage split I didn't see that much of her.

SUE: I didn't see anybody then. That wasn't Jane's fault. It wasn't anybody's fault, just the way it was. I was pretty traumatised and I probably went into hibernation. I didn't have any money, and I felt that terribly. I couldn't afford to go anywhere. Also, there were times when I actually liked being on my own at that stage.

JANE: Well, I didn't have the opportunity to find out what that was like because I had my present husband hovering around in the wings before I actually left home. I wouldn't have lived with him if I'd had an alternative. I wanted to be single, but I had no income whatsoever. I'd been getting the TEAS [Tertiary Education Assistance Scheme] allowance which had cut out in December, and I couldn't get Social Security because I hadn't sued my husband for maintenance . . . and there was my present husband saying: 'Why won't you come and live with me?' So what do you do? I like him, so I wasn't wrong in marrying him, but I never got that opportunity to find what I was looking for by myself, and I never will.

SUE: But you did like him. You didn't want to be without him.

JANE: Oh, yes, I remember thinking, *If only I could put him in a* cupboard for two years and know that he'd be there when I got back. I wanted that opportunity. I just didn't have it.

Here, Sue and Jane discussed the effect, if any, that their involvement with the group had on their relationships with children and new partners.

JANE: I don't think I relate differently to the kids. When the movement started the kids were only little. I have one boy and two girls, and I try to treat them the same but I can't say that I've done that. They make it very hard, because they're so different.

SUE: My son had to give a talk in year eleven, and the title was 'How Would You Like a Feminist for a Mother?' It was really funny. He said, 'You people just don't know what it's like'. He was aghast because he got the highest marks in the class.

JANE: And it was full of that typical male stuff about not getting your shirts ironed, and all the other things boys are supposed to get from their mothers. He kept complaining about it not being done for him. *(Collective groan and laughter.)*

My second marriage is significantly different from the first one, and the group was largely responsible for that. It was the best thing that ever happened to me because it set me on the path of changing my life. I chose differently. Before the women's movement I just accepted that you got married to whatever man came along and you had a very dreary life . . . you were a servant to the male. The second time around I wasn't prepared to accept that. I'd started bucking the system. So I haven't *made* my second husband different. I chose him because he *was* basically different. Oh, he has the occasional flash of chauvinistic attitude, but generally he's good.

SUE: Well, my present partner is the sort of person who always likes to be in control, and I guess I allow it most of the time. There's a power struggle between us. I'm glad I didn't meet him the first time around because the struggle would probably have been to the death. But I think it's something I can work out . . . It doesn't cause too many ripples because I like him. It was only four years ago [that the marriage ended]. This relationship's two years' old now.

As far as my relationship with the kids is concerned, the most difficult time for me was when I first left the marriage. The older boy decided that perhaps he should look after his father, which turned out to be a disaster, so I only had one son with me. The kids like my partner, but he's totally different from my ex-husband, different as chalk and cheese. It's a totally different atmosphere.

JANE: Having kids with a stepfather is not quite the same.

SOPHIA: He's still not the parent.

SUE: No, that's the hardest part of the relationship, I think. It's very difficult. My partner is not interested in any way.

SOPHIA: What's he like around the house?

SUE: He will always wash and iron but neither of us do it with much grace. I probably do more of it than he does because I'm home more. When we first met he was living on his own and doing all those things himself. I find he doesn't tend to do them as much as he used to. Not that he ever complains about it not being done, but . . . I'm home; he works longer hours. I still dig my heels in about that sort of thing. It makes me very angry, but if I feel put upon I let him know.

JANE: I used to find that ironing my present husband's shirts was a big issue for me. I didn't really think I should do them but I used to sort of bite my nails while he did them. I felt guilty, and he considered it my job. Even though he'd ironed them before I moved in with him, once I moved in it was like I was the shirt ironer. He doesn't say a word now, he does it automatically. But we went through a period where I felt quite uncomfortable. It's as much a matter of talking to yourself as it is of convincing them.

Here the women reflect on the ways in which their relationships with women outside the group were affected by what they experienced when they were in it.

SOPHIA: I think it made me respect women more, and made me see them as much more fragile. I learned that inside the together exterior there was a lot of damage.

You know, because of the intimacy of consciousness-raising, whenever I came across ordinary women . . . not feminists . . . they might have been dolly birds . . . I still sort of sensed that they were fragile people. And in the workplace I would always support them. It didn't matter how much they played up to a feminine role or did themselves a disservice, I'd always back them up in the face of chauvinism from the guys.

SUE: And I found that other women were surprised when they got that support. They weren't expecting it, because traditionally we've thought of ourselves as being in competition with other women.

JANE: Women are always judging other women like men do. I'd say that I don't do that now, whereas I might have done it before. But neither do I have any relationships with women.

I was thinking when you were talking that most of the time I'm working in areas that are dominated by men, and if there's the odd woman around I tend to avoid her. I feel sad about this . . . it's like . . . women are these weak little creatures and they associate with each other because they're intimidated by the men. And I won't be intimidated . . . so I won't sit with women. It's like going to the toilet with your girlfriends. And I don't want to be in that. But it's amazing how often they all seem to end up together. There will be a room full of a hundred men and three women and they always end up sitting side by side at the table, and I always wonder if they're deliberately clustering together or if the men have pushed them together . . . *(long pause)* . . . What I was thinking was that I deny women. I don't know what it is. I work in total isolation anyway. I'm under siege with those men and I don't even pass the time of day with the women.

SUE: I've got absolutely nothing in common with the ones at work. It's not really healthy, is it?

JANE: No. Every job should have a certain element of enjoyment and camaraderie and none exists there. Every so often I ring up that group, 'Women in Business', and I get their papers, but I never seem to progress any further.

SOPHIA: I work with women managers, and I love it, because they smile and get angry, and they get really emotional about stuff and have real arguments, and they don't lose any of their power or their competence.

SUE: Well, in my experience of working with women managers I found that some aspects of their behaviour are really male . . . their aggressiveness.

SOPHIA: Because they're proving themselves. You should recognise that.

SUE: Oh, I do. But then I look at the bitchiness in some of them and I wonder if it's necessary.

SOPHIA: But you have to understand . . .

SUE: I do, and I wouldn't notice it if it was a man. I expect it from a man, but I still have trouble coming to terms with it in a woman. I used to really feel that women were my best friends. I wanted to live with a woman. Partly because of all the conversations we had in the group. I felt that I could live with a woman forever and that life would be so much simpler.

SOPHIA: There is something very fundamental, isn't there? That commonality with your own gender.

JANE: It could also have been that we didn't know many men that we liked at the time. When it comes down to it, are there many now?

SUE: Oh, I'd hate to think there weren't.

SOPHIA: I actually think there are two races on this earth. A male race and a female race. Now, I'm just getting myself together after breaking up with someone, and I'm meeting lots of really great men. It's incredible . . . but they're different. I can still fall in love with a man, sleep with him, live with him, have kids and all the rest of it, but it's different. Two different races, and no one will ever convince me otherwise.

The women seemed to agree with Sue's comment that 'You can't say one's better than the other'. As a rule, and contrary to what many people believed at the time, the groups didn't indulge in much verbal man-bashing. The women had been preoccupied with other issues. Here they were asked to remember which of those issues had been most important to them in the '70s.

SOPHIA: They were material/political issues. I got involved in the class analysis of society, the Vietnam War, the ecology movement, all that sort of stuff.

The personal/sexual issues were there too . . . the whole women's liberation thing about your personal life being a result of decisions that had been made for you, or that society, the media or whatever, had pressured you into. And it was the whole issue of sexuality too. But the big thing for me was *changing the world*.

SUE: The big thing for me was *me*. I was married with two kids, and I was just surviving. I was really in trouble. I couldn't go into a room full of people without screeching.

JANE: Well, I couldn't deal with the world if I couldn't find a baby-sitter. I knew there was some reason why it was always *me* who had to find the baby-sitter, but that was the limit of my social perspective.

SUE: I never really did much about external issues. I remember I went on one march and a demonstration, but I could never have protested on the trams. Remember that?

JANE: That was when we were campaigning for equal pay for women.* You know, they were paid less, but charged the same for fares. So we staged a protest.

SUE: Well, I thought that was terrific but I couldn't do it.

JANE: In those days they still had separate rooms for women in pubs and I remember a bunch of us storming a public bar insisting on being served. I didn't really want to go in there anyway. *(Laughs.)* It was all happening around the same time.

I remember when we staged a sit-in at the office of the Minister for Housing, Mr. Dickie. It was about conditions in Housing Commission flats. There had been a spate of people falling from windows and being killed. Anyway, I got a shock because the women who actually lived in the flats resented us being there. I was really put back in my box. I thought we were supporting working-class women but apparently *they* were saying: 'Don't patronise us'.

SUE: Yes, 'What would you know about our situation. Piss off!' I felt good about going there, demonstrating this new sense of solidarity. But we really got slapped in the face, because they said: 'Who asked you?' Actually, that was one of the things the women's movement really opened up for me . . . an awareness of class.

Asked if the same issues preoccupy them today, Sophia is quick to say: 'No!'

SOPHIA: I still feel very strongly about violence toward women. And this talk now of reversing the abortion laws . . . I thought we'd sorted this out years ago, and now I think, *Don't tell me I do have to go and walk the streets again.* I don't want to do it . . . Things about equal pay don't get me, but the biology stuff . . . it just makes me see red.

I don't have any involvement now in anything that's organised

---

* Equal pay for women became law only in 1972.

political. I've had opportunities from time to time . . . friends who try to drag me back into it. I've got one friend who tries to drag me along to women's balls and I think, *oh, puke!* Yeah, I just burnt out.

SUE: Does that mean you still feel stirred up about all those things, but you just aren't on committees anymore, or does none of that stuff matter to you?

SOPHIA: It's not that it doesn't matter. I just feel now that it's somebody else's struggle. I gave, from the age of eighteen to the age of thirty at least . . . twelve years . . . basically a hundred percent of my life. Newsletters and this march and that organisation. You know, I just put everything into it. My sexuality . . . I went into sleeping with women and everything. So when I hit thirty-one I woke up and I thought, *I just want to try and see the world differently. I just want something different.*

SUE: Is that when your anger sort of subsided?

SOPHIA: I think my anger subsided because I put more energy into my career and I was successful. Fortunately through the women's movement I learned leadership and organisational skills which contributed thousands of dollars to my life.

But I think I just became, and still am, a very assertive person, a very strong person. And I still have to get a lot of it out of my system, because it's affected my relationships with men. I can see how I'm constantly doing things wrong, things that upset them. Recently an old flame contacted me, and when he arrived I'd already organised the restaurant, the wine we were going to drink and what we were going to do afterwards. Well, he just said: 'You haven't changed'. I'm don't let the other person have a say because I'm used to thinking nobody's going to tell me which restaurant I should go to because I'm a woman.

Now I really want a successful relationship with a man. But I keep mucking it up with all this organising ability. You know, 'We're doing it this way and you come along'. As though they were ancillary. And I don't know what to do about it.

SUE: So, if somebody asked you if you were a feminist now what would you say?

SOPHIA: I'd still say yes, but I don't volunteer it. I don't act like I used to, jumping on every comment somebody makes.

SUE: No, I don't either. *(They laugh.)*

JANE: I think the only issue for me was sorting myself out, and getting equality for myself, and that's still important.

SOPHIA: Did you sort it out?

JANE: No. My personal life is alright, but I work in a very male-dominated organisation and I find that I'm being challenged in that area all the time. To the extent that I'm coming across as an aggressive feminist. I'm not aware of it . . . I don't think I am . . . but people tell me that I am.

SUE: The work issue is still there for me too. I mean, women still get paid less and no amount of talking about it has changed the rules. I'm currently changing my job because of this very issue.

Pay equity between men and women in Australia is a myth. according to a report by the National Women's Consultative Council. The report, launched on 8 August 1990 by the Minister for Industrial Relations, states that women earn on average 65% of what male employees earn. Even though women must legally receive the same pay for the same job, the study points out that industries in which women predominate pay less than male-dominated industries, and women have less access to over-time and over-award payments. Lynne Cossar, 'Equality in pay is a myth . . .', The Age, 9 August 1990.

At this point Sophia said she was curious about whether group members had maintained contact with each other over the years, given that she 'went west' and hadn't seen anybody else in a long time. This was a lead in to her asking whether Sue or Jane had experienced misgivings, as she had, about getting together again, or about the book in general. She went on to explain.

SOPHIA: I think I just didn't want to recreate those years of my life. I'd been there, done that, left it all behind. And I didn't want to experience déjà vu. I don't like repeating my cycles, especially now when I'm heading into my forties. I want a sense of newness in the next decade. So when I was contacted I was really hesitant. And I backed out of the weekend away.

At the same time, the reason I agreed to be interviewed was because of an enormous sense of owing something to the people who contributed to my development. And the people in the group did contribute, just by allowing me to listen to what was happening in their lives. Obviously, I was talking about my life as well, and I was contributing to everybody else who listened to what I was saying. So there was a genuine feeling that I owed it. I owed it back.

SUE: Yes, that's true for me too. But I think my new partner had misgivings. I think it was because he knew that had been a very unsettled period of my life. A lot happened during that time.

SOPHIA: It was so significant. Somebody wanted to do something with me tonight, actually. And I said: 'Oh, no, I'm going to see my CR group!'

SUE: Nobody I've said that to knew what a CR group was.

SOPHIA: Yeah, well that's a sign of the times, isn't it?

JANE: Well, I didn't have any misgivings at all. I enjoyed the whole episode and I was really happy to come back and think about it some more.

SUE: Yes, I liked what Sophia said about storing up all that history. You don't think about it again until somebody asks you. And then you remember.

SOPHIA: The other thing is that it distinguishes you from the rest.

Really when you look back you have a story to tell. It's in the fabric of your life, and people say: 'Oooah, you were one of *them?*'

The conversation took on an historical perspective, with the women comparing the commitment and energy of the early days to a certain complacency and lack of focus in the present. Sue and Sophia were especially concerned that the next generation of young women will assume there is nothing left to fight for, and will ultimately come up hard against a new conservatism as the penalty for their lack of vigilance.

SUE: The abortion issue is a perfect example. We can't assume that we've got it made for all time. Somebody's always ready to snatch it away from us.

SOPHIA: Also, I think the society we rebelled against was a very materialistic one. And now, because people are saturated with consumer products they seem to be moving towards the less tangible values. The romantic movement seems to be coming back, in the sense of family and children . . . the dream life . . . and I think it's a trap.

SUE: It moves a woman back again into a particular role.

SOPHIA: Exactly. They might have the right to be everywhere now . . . in the clubs and the pubs and the board rooms . . . but at the same time there's a particular style . . . a mode emerging . . . which is eventually going to put women into that feminine, romantic . . . kind of pre-Raphaelite thing. I look at the girls in the clubs and discos, and they're all in these flat shoes and bobby sox. It's the little girl look, and they're all in their twenties. So I think that's where things are shifting. And there's the New Right as well.

SUE: And sex is out because of AIDS.

SOPHIA: Right. So your assertion in terms of your sexuality is going. And maybe it will only be right again within the marriage with one partner, and you can't explore anything much any more.

The discussion eventually turned to what had been the women's dreams for the future during their teenage years. There was a great deal of laughter induced by memories of starry-eyed fantasies.

SUE: I was going to be a nurse who gave my husband orange juice in bed. Or I could have been a hairdresser. Actually, giving my husband orange juice was my idea of marriage. But I never saw any farther than breakfast.

JANE: You never thought about the washing up?

SUE: Never. I'd seen my brother and his wife having breakfast together when they were first married, and they smiled across the table to each other. It was so romantic. My mother used to say: 'For goodness sake, just think about it. The man you sit across the breakfast table from — that's it!'

SOPHIA: When I was a teenager I wanted to be married at thirty-eight, and have two kids, a girl and a boy. My mother got married at thirty-eight. I never questioned why. Maybe it was the war.

JANE: But that took some of the pressure off you to hurry up and get married?

SOPHIA: Yeah, it did. Even though Mum and Dad did the whole thing when I was sixteen of bringing in the Italian farmer from Mansfield with a hundred head of cattle and a vegetable garden and all the rest of it. You know, he was forty-five. And I said: 'No'.

SUE: Do you want to have kids?

SOPHIA: Yes. *(She gives a short laugh.)* I'm one year off thirty-eight. I'm leaving it a bit late.

JANE: I had a picture of marriage which was to do with . . . um . . . matched tableware. That was important. Having nice matched tableware. Before I got married, somewhere along the line — and I didn't expect I would ever achieve my aspirations — I thought I would like to be famous for writing a technical book, on mathematics or something like that. I don't know why. That was when I was a bit older than a teenager. I always thought five children would be a nice number to have.

SUE: Actually, none of them would have survived if she'd had five.

Interview 4: 10 July 1989
Rose

After the CR group ended, Rose lost touch with the other women, except for Sue whom she continued to meet for a while. When we contacted her about the reunion she was excited by the prospect of seeing everyone again. But when it came to being interviewed, it was always difficult for her to find a time when she could join one of the others. Finally we arranged to speak with her by herself in a city office one afternoon after work. What follows is Rose's account of those early days and the impact of the group on her life.

I was from the country originally, and I was a Labor voter. *(Rose laughs as though this explains a great deal about her.)* I had always believed I was strange. When I read Germaine Greer's book I realised that I wasn't really. Before that I had thought there must be more to life . . . more than being married and having kids. Cooking wasn't enough for me. I wanted to keep on learning.

And I thought I was strange because of all these silly thoughts . . . that I was different from other women. When I read Greer's book it changed my whole life. For the first time somebody was putting down on paper how I felt. When I read it I thought, *My God, that woman is writing about me!*

Then I came to Melbourne and discovered all that was going on here. I didn't go and burn my bra. But I became aware of women's rights . . . and about how I felt inside sort of . . . about relationships. It wasn't political . . . it was just being aware.

I can't remember how I first heard about the group. I think I rang the Switchboard and they put me on to it. I found that first meeting very hard. The trouble was, I'd never been close to women before . . . I would never even have said something like that in the country . . . It was like bearing wounds. That was something I wasn't used to doing. It was very different for me.

But everyone seemed to like me. I didn't have to talk about kids and curtains. I realised I wasn't going to upset anybody. And later when I had that abortion I really needed their support. Nobody condemned you in that group.

I didn't have close relationships with women outside the group. It was in the group that I discovered I could confide in women about anything. I didn't have to think twice about what I said. So then I started to be more open with women outside the group and in return they started being more open with me. Especially regarding sex.

It's still hard for me to express myself. Perhaps I used to listen more than talk in the group. I think I used to get a bit overawed . . . overwhelmed. But I wouldn't have kept going if I'd felt I didn't belong. I don't suppose it actually changed me a great deal. It was more that we were able to express ourselves. And it's interesting . . . I think in our group we *stayed* ourselves. We weren't influenced by the conformity of the bigger Movement.

I didn't actually get any opposition from my family about the group. They weren't hostile . . . just a bit cynical. They just thought I'd gone a bit strange. But I did talk to my daughter about what I was doing. And I took her to a women's clinic when she wouldn't see a doctor. And I got her a copy of *Our Bodies, Ourselves*.* The group influenced my ideas on how to bring up children. It made me more broadminded.

If it had influenced me *more* I'd have done something back then about my marriage. It wasn't a real marriage and I really wasn't

---

* Boston Women's Health Book Collective, New York, Simon & Schuster, 1973, revised 1976.

happy. I would have loved to walk out, but the kids came first . . . and I was too scared of poverty. Or maybe it was just laziness, because I was more or less left alone to do what I wanted. I'm sure if it had become unbearable I would have gone.

The partner, who I live with now, is different from any man I've known before. He's considerate of me. He treats me like a woman. *(Rose holds her fingers up to indicate quotation marks, and laughs.)* He brings me flowers. That probably means I'm not much of a feminist. But, you know, there's a big difference between thirty and fifty.

Here Rose reflects on the issues which aroused her in the '70s, and on what matters to her now.

They were personal issues mainly . . . In those days it was hard to do anything as a woman. You couldn't get a bank loan, or a bankcard in your own name. You didn't have the same freedom as a man. My father had said to me: 'Your place is in the home. Have more kids instead of going out to work.' But I didn't feel that I was supposed to stay at home and look after kids all my life.

The main social issue for me was equal pay. I used to be active in the Union. I even became a shop steward. I'd like to be able to get fanatical the way I did back then. But I never do anything anymore. When you're working ten-hour shifts you lose touch. These days women have to worry about 'male' stress — heart attacks and nervous breakdowns.

I was more politically aware then than I am now. Of course the political parties have changed these days; Labor is the same as Liberal. Also . . . maybe it's my age . . . I'm a grandmother now. I'm more interested in the environment. And nuclear war, and animal liberation. And domestic violence and child abuse.

In my job, I've got what I wanted . . . promotion. But I'm still considered 'just a woman'. If I get cross at work about something that shouldn't have happened, they say I'm being 'emotional' which means a typical woman. And I've discovered how chauvinistic the Union is. That came as quite a surprise to me because theoretically it fights for women's rights. But when it comes to really doing something for the women, you find the Union's just a men's club, representing men's interests. Still, I defend women in the workplace.

If someone asked me whether I was a feminist today, I'd say no. It was clear what a feminist was in those days. What *is* a feminist today? I don't know. In those days things were changing. I loved that era. It was an important part of history. Now the changes have happened. What do we ask for today?

Notes

Each woman had joined the CR group because she was unhappy about some aspect of her life. Some saw women's liberation as one manifestation of a worldwide climate of revolution, or an agent for change in the areas which most concerned them. Others were on a journey of self-discovery.

The pursuit of different agendas, those stated and those only vaguely understood by the individuals themselves, did create occasional tension between members. There were ideological conflicts and personality clashes, but in spite of these, the women all regarded the CR group as an environment in which it had been safe to disagree.

Functionally the consciousness-raising group was a success because it did what the women had wanted it to do: it raised their consciousness of both personal and wider political issues. And while friendship was a secondary consideration in the group, an unprecedented intimacy and bonding existed among its members.

It was the non-judgemental nature of the CR group which seems to have been its greatest appeal. In interviews this emerged as a key issue. The women believed that all women are constantly being scrutinised, assessed and compared to each other, to some idealised image of womanhood, and to men.

They made many references to the destructive impact on their self-esteem of a lifelong sense of being evaluated according to behaviour, appearance and ideas, by everyone from family and friends to strangers and other women in the movement. In contrast, they had felt themselves accepted in the group. This had made it possible for them to communicate without fear of being ostracised. Many regarded this freedom as the first step in their process towards liberation.

It is impossible to make simple statements about where the women placed themselves within Australian society at the time they belonged to the CR group. Any such discussion must take into consideration a number of contributing factors, not the least of which may have been their strong desire for the group to survive.

Relationships among the members of the group were so important that after it disbanded some of them never again attained that level of connection with other women.

We said the women hadn't joined the group, or the movement, to find friends. Nevertheless, they'd had great expectations of each other and faith in the concept of sisterhood. Therefore it is not surprising that some of them had been bitterly disappointed to discover that gender experience alone didn't create solidarity. Some expressed lingering feelings of pain and anger at having had their life choices censured by factions in the wider movement.

At the same time they attributed their defiance of this perceived exclusion to precisely those ideals inherent in the women's liberation philosophy which encouraged women to make appropriate choices for themselves.

Group members had been forced to let go of their romantic illusions about the unity of women, but in doing so they had made discoveries about the factors, such as class and race, which divide women.

Oddly, class was never acknowledged as a determining factor in relationships within the group, only outside it. This was so even though the women were aware of, and often discussed, the considerable differences in members' backgrounds, educations and incomes. It is possible that individuals within the group analysed its dynamics from a class-based perspective, but it was never done openly as a group exercise.

It is equally possible that, perhaps unconsciously, the women chose to view their differences as simply experiential, rather than risk any tension which a class-based interpretation of those differences might have engendered.

Though much of the group's time was taken up with discussion of ideological issues, there seems never to have been any questioning of party-political allegiances among the members. No doubt because of the A.L.P.'s stated commitment to social justice, there was an assumption that everyone in the group voted Labor.

This closing of ranks and sense of group cohesiveness is particularly interesting when seen alongside the women's perception of themselves as marginalised by the wider movement.

Also, several of the women underwent significant changes in education, income and lifestyle following the disbanding of the group, and tended in interviews to reflect these changes. For example, Jane talks about her initial impression 'that the movement was only for the educated middle class'. Later she describes her ascendancy to a top executive position within her corporation, and confesses that these days she 'denies women' because she doesn't want to be identified with them.

Most of the women continued to have important friendships with other women. Some actually preferred the company of women to that of men; they felt practically, intellectually and emotionally sustained by wide networks of women. There seemed to be agreement that whatever their differences women generally share more common ground with each other than they do with men. As Sophia said, 'there are two races on this earth.'

Some group members felt that, for various reasons, they did not have as much contact with other women as they would like. There was the suggestion that a woman who achieves success in the world of business or politics is necessarily separated from other women, that her status is threatened by association with 'the girls'.

Sophia, the youngest member of the group, stated that consciousness-raising had contributed to her development by giving her intimate insights into the lives of other women, women whom she probably would not have known in any other context.

In a later chapter she recalls what it had felt like to watch these apparently conservative women undergoing profound changes in their relationships with themselves, their partners and families, and the rest of their world. She had noted at the time that personal, internal change was a political act.

The greatest aid to change seems to have been, for all the women, the group's function as an information exchange. They talked of having been empowered by meetings fired with anecdotes and statistics on everything from sex and health to government policies on education and childcare.

Many of the women cited the reassurance of normality they gained as an important by-product of information. Agnes in particular credited the group with introducing her to a social and historical context in which to examine many of the problems she had previously considered evidence of personal flaws. Gloria also talked about her fear prior to joining the group that she was 'mad or bad'. Rose said she had always believed she was 'strange'. When questioned, Rose felt that the group had not changed her so much as it had allowed her to feel good about herself as she was.

We asked the women to tell us what dreams and ambitions they had grown up with. Most of them admitted aspirations which had been either modest or ill-defined. Those who had harboured ideas of something grander than a future as a housewife had tended to laugh at themselves for being unrealistic.

Jane, Gloria and Helen linked the confidence and self-esteem they gained in the group with their decision to further their education, which in turn had created career possibilities and financial independence, which had further enhanced their confidence. But all the women were careful to point out that a contributing factor in this spiral was their maturity.

There seems to have been real ignorance on the part of some husbands, relatives and friends about the philosophies of women's liberation and the rationale behind consciousness-raising. Reactions to the women's membership in the group, particularly from husbands, had been complex, ranging from encouragement, indifference and embarrassment to hostility and defensiveness. Sometimes there had been awkward combinations of all of these.

The women had indicated by their behaviour, interests, sometimes speech and appearance that they were undergoing changes. In and out of interviews, they told us about their partners and others 'noticing that something was happening' and in most cases feeling threatened by it, but not immediately linking it to consciousness-raising.

When the men finally realised there was a connection some had responded by blaming the group for their failed marriages. Some had been unable to differentiate between a group where marital problems were created, and one where they were merely discussed along with other issues. The women made it clear that they attributed the high incidence of divorce among them to bad marriages rather than to membership in a disruptive group.

A few husbands had shown support in principle for their wives, even though in practice they had occasionally trembled as the ground shifted beneath them. One had initially imagined an advantage in having a feminist wife who would relieve him of the responsibility for financially supporting his family.

But others had seen their wife going to meetings — any kind of meetings — as an act of rebellion in itself. They had been less concerned about where she went, or why, than about her 'secrecy' and her willingness to 'desert the family'. Predictably, there had been the ubiquitous accusations of lesbian orgies, which suggested just how alarming and bewildering some men found the idea of friendship between women.

Some of the women seem to have had trouble integrating the group experience with the rest of their lives. Helen felt it desirable to keep her CR comrades separate from her husband and ordinary social life, convinced that mixing them could cause trouble. Gloria spoke of the pressure of leading a double life, of trying to maintain a role outside the group, where she was expected to carry on as daughter, wife, mother.

It wasn't hard to understand why women in transition would need to compartmentalise their activities, but it could be argued that they were doing more than simply balancing old lives with new ones. There were suggestions that not all the pressure was being exerted from outside the group. For instance, Gloria referred to her distress over being told by a group member to 'go bake cakes'. Sue admitted changing her shoes before meetings, to 'get the image right' and after one taped session, Jane reminded Agnes that she had once confessed to owning two wardrobes: one for women's lib and one for the rest of her life.

So just how confident were the women of the acceptance the group offered? Was their need to dress the part a habit formed by years of conditioning about the relationship between appearance and acceptability? Was it proof of shallow personalities playing 'Women's Liberationist' as one of many roles in a repertoire? Was it evidence of their insecurity about whether they really belonged in a movement where they were often criticised for their conservatism? Or was donning the trappings simply an outward way of expressing a new inner state; was it in fact a legitimate aid to a ritual shift in consciousness?

Unfortunately we can only ask the questions, not answer them. This issue wasn't examined in any detail during the interviews. In fact it only emerged as an issue after the interviews were completed, and we noticed recurring, often humorous, references to the need to present an appropriate image in the company of women who belonged to the movement.

One negative but powerful image which attached itself to the label 'feminist' back in the '70s, and which to some extent haunts it today, was that of the aggressive, insensitive, uncompromising, man-hating, humourless and unrealistic (usually lesbian) woman with a shaved head and overalls. This was discussed, and will be taken up in more depth in a later chapter.

How things have changed

In which the women discuss: new partners; old expectations; independence; communication; balance of power; stepfathers; retirement; women-only events; women friends; the sensitive male; fear; ageing and ageism; achievement; authority figures; abortion; money, and much more.

Interview 1: 4 February 1990
Rita, Gloria, Helen and Agnes

These interviews were held at Kristin's house on a warm Sunday in February. Over a long lunch, with several bottles of wine, Agnes, Helen, Gloria and Rita filled in the years between 1974, when the group had ceased to meet, and today. Unfortunately, this was the final contribution from Rita. A couple of weeks after this session she decided to withdraw from the project. We had no choice but to accept her decision, but we did this with regret and disappointment. Rita's willingness to talk about her experiences, both in and out of the CR group, had been invaluable.

The sort of things the women discussed in this interview had been suggested in letters circulated to them prior to the meeting. They arrived ready to share their ideas about relationships with partners, families and the world at large, and especially with themselves. They explained how both the ideas and the relationships had changed over the years.

GLORIA: I'll start by saying that I'm certainly trying to have a better relationship. Mainly it's him responding to the effort that *I'm* making. It's coming from me first, but I'm much more aware and much happier about it. I'm getting recognised as an individual . . . as a person . . . whereas in the first marriage I was just a chattel. *(Pause.)* My expectations have changed. They're probably not as high, or romantic, or schoolgirlish. I think I'm just much more practical in what I expect from a relationship. And I think mostly I'm satisfied.

RITA: I guess I still have the starry-eyed expectations, you know. I sometimes wonder if I could get somebody who was born on the same day and the same time and the same place as me, if we could sort of read each other's minds and basically see eye to eye.

The difference between my old marriage and my new relationship is the two people. They're quite different . . . probably opposites. My husband was very much the artist-come-academic. My present partner isn't literary at all. He's very numbers oriented . . . very aware of money and its value. Comparing the two, I don't think I am any better at having myself understood now than I was back then, and that's what I was hoping for.

HELEN: Do you feel that you're on an equal basis now?

RITA: No, not psychologically.

AGNES: What's your communication like with your present partner? You and your husband used to talk a lot, didn't you?

RITA: Right. At least when I was married it was possible to have a good discussion with my husband about something . . . as long as it was totally outside our relationship. We could go on for hours and hours philosophising about world hunger, or religion . . . but when it came down to tin tacks, about us together, it would usually just work out the same way as it does with my partner now.

I think the current relationship is probably a little more

intimate than my marriage was. We have the occasional hassle that sort of sets us apart . . . but you know . . . you have to snap back into it.

GLORIA: It's interesting . . . that it hasn't been a matter of finding the ideal man, but rather . . .

HELEN: . . . changing ourselves. Yes, I know I decided if I wanted improvement *I* had to change. Not so that I feel humiliated or as if I'm the loser. It's just that I have taken control.

RITA: I was just thinking of my interests outside the home. My partner doesn't seem to have any now that he's semi-retired, but I take it for granted that I'm going out at least once a week. He's come with me a few times, but he complains about smoke-filled rooms and he doesn't like drinking away from home because of the driving. We live further away from the city than we used to so it takes an hour to get anywhere, and he'd rather buy the booze and drink it in his own house than go out, even if I drove him. But still, once a week I want to go out.

HELEN: Does it bother him that you go out by yourself?

RITA: Well, I meet a girlfriend who has a lot of the same friends and likes the same places I do. I think he feels that if she's there I won't play up . . . that if I was going to play up I'd only do it by myself.

AGNES: It sounds like you've made a separate life for yourself. That's something that was always important to you, wasn't it?

RITA: Well, when I was married I went to Labor Party meetings, I went to CR meetings, I went to university . . .

GLORIA: So you've kept your independence.

RITA: Yes, but I think my partner resents it. He won't come right out and say so, but he slips things into arguments, little insinuations. He'd never admit that he feels insecure, or suggest that because he's broken away from the life we had in the city I should stop going back to it.

We never made a deal . . . we never said that the basis of our relationship was that we both had to give up all our former relationships . . . even with my sons. *(Here Rita explains that at one stage her younger son's living arrangements changed and he asked if he could stay with her for a few weeks.)* When I told him, his first reaction was: 'I'll go and stay in a motel while he's here'. I was absolutely shocked that he could say something like that. And since then he brings it up in arguments. As though I want to move him out and move my kids in . . . *(pause)* . . . And I think it's even worse since we've bought this house together. I sold my flat and he sold his house so we could pay for this. But I think it helped our relationship before for him to know that he had a place of his own.

AGNES: I've heard people say that even if they never use it . . . just knowing that they have an escape route . . .

RITA: Yes. But it doesn't take much to give me an escape. I can go away in the car for a couple of hours. And when I come back it's okay. I don't need long escapes . . . just frequent ones.

GLORIA: I think I've come to the conclusion that anybody else's shortcomings are their problem. And that makes it much easier to accept when other people let me down. That's been happening a lot recently with the family, and where once I would have been hysterical, now I'm coping. I asked myself if it was because I was just too tired to care, but . . . no, it's because I'm more accepting.

RITA: Well, I guess I'm not really all that different. I've seen a lot more and I've heard and experienced a lot more, and some of that's made me think, *Jeez, is life really like that!* But . . . I don't know . . . I've sort of expected most of what I've experienced. That's not to say life has been dull, because it hasn't.

AGNES: I definitely have a more intimate relationship now; it would have been hard to have a less intimate one than I had when I was married. I'm sometimes surprised at how little my husband and I knew each other. I think of myself as somebody who really likes to be close to people, but I actually lived with a man for twelve years and I didn't know him and he didn't know me. If you'd asked us, we would have said that we were quite close. But certainly now I experience a really satisfying sense of knowing my partner, and being known by him. And that includes mutual tolerance.

I think my expectations have changed. I identify very much with Gloria . . . I'm not so starry-eyed anymore. I always felt in my first marriage that what was missing was that overwhelming sense of passion. Well, I don't have that now either, but I don't want it. I've experienced it a few times and it didn't do me much good.

For the most part I'm really happy. And I'm proud of this relationship . . . that we're living up to values I hold, like not being jealous of each other. I guess I still hang out for the ease of communication that I have with my women friends. I still hope that one of these days, if we keep working at it, he'll become an easy talker. But after ten years, I don't know how likely that is.

GLORIA: When you say you haven't achieved that level of communication you'd like, is it because you're frightened to hurt his feelings?

AGNES: No, it's because I can't make him talk.

GLORIA: Oh, so the problem's coming from him. You're reaching out but he's not co-operating.

AGNES: Yes. I've learned to shut up though. I used to want to push all the time. It's the kind of thing you only notice when there's a problem. I don't expect us to sit around talking about how happy we are. But when there's a problem I need to talk about it to get some kind of resolution. Whereas he needs to get away from it. Also, I've discovered that we talk very differently. For instance, when we do talk on an issue . . . at some point in the discussion something clicks in his head and he thinks, *Oh, good, we've resolved that . . . it's over*. I don't hear the click, so I keep on talking, and then he goes from being reasonable to being angry, because he thought it was resolved and I wouldn't shut up about it. So I'm aware of the difference in the way we understand things. It's only fairly recently that I've figured this out, and I'm thinking I should say to him: 'Next time you hear that click, tell me, because I *don't* hear it'.

He's never going to turn into somebody who wants to 'get into things' and consequently, I don't want to get into them as much as I used to . . . I probably couldn't go into a CR group the way I did before, because I don't have the same need I had then, to pull things apart and examine them. I don't know . . . maybe that's a phase we all went through in the '70s, after centuries of not talking.

GLORIA: Yes, I think it was, because I don't need to talk anywhere near as much.

AGNES: I do have one other expectation, and this is sheer fantasy. The kids laugh at me about this one. They say I want us to be the Brady Bunch, and we're not, and we never will be. Sometimes my son and my partner can't speak to each other. They have a level of peaceful co-existence which depends on staying out of each other's way. But I wanted everybody I love to love each other, and I fought against them not doing that for years. I still have to remind myself that it's not going to happen. But, the more you say that to yourself, the more it sinks in.

GLORIA: If you start talking about that step-parenting thing it could go on for ever. You open up a whole can of worms. Because when you go into a second relationship it's not just the person-to-person relationship you get, but also you bring your family and you get theirs. And the person who bears the brunt of things is usually the mother.

HELEN: Well, I decided to stay in my marriage. When all my women friends, inside and outside the group, started having marriage break-ups I sat down and asked myself: 'Why is this happening? Is this what I want too?' I went through a time when I thought I might leave, but I started looking at what I wanted and what I had . . . the positives and negatives . . . and I decided to stay.

I knew I couldn't change my partner, but I didn't need to take on his problems. It was up to me to control what *I* did. So I've stayed in the relationship, but I constantly reassess it. What suits me now might not suit me in a few years, and I know if the time comes when I can't accept being in it anymore I can go. This is what I have done ever since that decision to stay in the marriage. It's all up to me. I'm not going to be influenced by anything around me.

And I think what helped me was talking in the group, and reading about men. I came to the conclusion that they have a hard lot too. I mean, they're not what they're made out to be. When you look a bit deeper . . . scratch a bit . . . you see they're as vulnerable as we are. So I won't be bluffed by their bullying. Sometimes my husband tries to sound like the great authority on things, but I see through it. I know it's just an act to keep the image up. I look at him and I think, *I'm not going to be frightened* and that has helped me.

GLORIA: It sounds like you weighed everything up very carefully.

HELEN: Yes, I did. And I still do. I take a year at a time. This way I don't feel that I've made any decisions that I'll have to abide by forever. But at the moment, the arrangement suits me. I've learned to think about what I like, without being too selfish. My husband goes diving, and I hate the sea. So I made up my mind really early that I wouldn't go with him. Why should I spend my weekends doing something I hate? And once I got over this, things worked much better. If I listen to myself, and compromise where I can, and I don't compromise where I can't . . . then I don't end up resenting him. If I give in on something then it's my own fault. I believe I'm in control.

Helen's concern about being in control of her life led to a discussion on something the women had been asked to consider: the distribution of power within their relationships.

AGNES: I'm the head of the family because my kids live with us and the house is mine. That's not so important now that we've been together ten years, but it was very important to me in the beginning and it must have been hard for him. He definitely joined an existing unit.

The more an issue concerns both of us, the more equally we share the power. But in the day-to-day stuff I'm organising for three-quarters of the family and he's organising for one. I'd say I have power over myself, and responsibility for my children.

HELEN: Well, the power, if that's the right word, has changed a bit since my husband has retired and I'm still working. My perception of myself has changed, and things are more equal.

GLORIA: Yes, I understand that because the same thing has happened to me.

AGNES: Has it got to do with the fact that you're earning money and he isn't?

HELEN: I don't know . . . I haven't figured it out yet. I just feel more equal.

GLORIA: You feel more of a useful person in society than he is. You're the one who's contributing to society.

HELEN: That's it exactly. I had failed to recognise how much power there is in being part of the paid workforce . . . and how little power there is if you're at home, even if you've accumulated a lot of money from before. It's a funny thing . . . and a sad thing . . . and it doesn't matter whether you're male or female . . . work at home is still not valued.

AGNES: Do you two realise what you're saying?

GLORIA: I know, and it's terrible, but I feel exactly the same.

HELEN: I always thought that that attitude was wrong . . . and yet now I make these remarks about people who sit around all day doing nothing. Of course, he isn't sitting around. He's doing further education, and he's also doing half the housework.

AGNES: My god, this is incredible! Look at the days when we were taking care of the house. Now, listening to you I know that it wouldn't have mattered how hard we worked as long as it wasn't outside the home. We never had a hope of being valued the same way our husbands were.

HELEN: Exactly, and I've turned around.

GLORIA: We're doing the same thing to them that they did to us.

HELEN: Well, it's more than just that. I can't help resenting the fact that he doesn't leave the house in the morning and stay away till the evening. That was always a very safe time for me, from nine to five. For twenty-eight years I was used to having that time for myself, and now there's somebody there reading the paper, and somebody in the shower when I want to take one. He's taking my space up. I used to always make sure I came home ten minutes early, to be by myself before the rest of the family got home . . . and often I can't do that now. I resent it. There are things about his retirement that haven't been sorted out yet . . .

RITA: I never gave it much thought when my partner said he was going to retire. I know he wanted to. If he's happy, then I'm happy. If it's bothering him, then it bothers me. Anyway, there really hasn't been that much change. He had a consultancy practice which wasn't a nine-to-five job. People used to come to the house and there were lots of phone calls all the time and I was there because I wasn't working.

At this point Rita referred again to the question of intimacy, pointing out that we hadn't actually discussed sexual intimacy, and that it was different from the kind of closeness we had been talking about.

RITA: My husband would have said that he never made any sexual demands on me when we were married. But that's a kind of demand in itself. I get different kinds of demands now. My present partner expresses them, verbally and physically. The situation's the same, just at a different level.

AGNES: Do you mean because the demands are more out in the open?

RITA: Well, yes, although sometimes the motives behind his demands are hidden. With him, I try not to do anything dangerous. I did dangerous things when I was married, because I thought my husband didn't care. I don't do that now.

GLORIA: You mean, trying to make him jealous?

RITA: Oh, he is jealous anyway, without me doing anything. He is definitely sexually jealous. My husband would have said that he wasn't jealous, and he never appeared to be.

AGNES: When you say 'dangerous' do you mean in terms of the stability of your relationship, or would he actually . . . get physically violent.

RITA: No, he's never been violent . . . not physically violent . . . with me, but from what he says of his past life, he's capable of physical violence. He says he's controlling himself, and I believe him. It doesn't take much to start an argument. So I try not to say anything that may sound controversial. Anything controversial is dangerous, unless it coincides with his opinion. I don't talk about feminism. I did in the past and he got quite upset. It intimidates him.

AGNES: Does he know you're doing this interview today?

RITA: Oh, yes. The letter was out on the coffee table; he read it. And he even spoke to Marlene on the phone. It seems to be okay just so long as I don't do anything too overt, like go to a demonstration or something, and be taken in by the police or get on the television news.

AGNES: So, you know what the rules are that you mustn't break?

RITA: Yes.

GLORIA: That's awful!

HELEN: Oh, I don't know. There are certain things in my life that I don't talk about with my husband. Feminism is one of them. There are parts of my life that have nothing to do with him, just like there are parts of his life I don't want to know about.

AGNES: But there's a hell of difference between maintaining the right not to disclose every thought and action to a partner, and actually being afraid that the disclosure could end up causing you bodily harm.

This was an uncomfortable point in the discussion. Although the women communicated in an overall atmosphere of tolerance for each other's opinions, there was still sometimes ideological friction between them, often stemming from concerns about the different levels of compromise each found acceptable.

AGNES: Well, in our house feminism isn't a private conviction. I think we actually live in a feminist household. I don't know how much that's because I've insisted on it and how much it's because my partner thinks it's a natural way to live. He accepts a lot of things that aren't traditional, and I think that's possibly his age. He's considerably younger than your partners.

GLORIA: It's age, but I'm sure it's the individual as well.

HELEN: Well, when you say that, I think our house is feminist too. Some people who visit us notice that perhaps it's a bit different. I saw this when another couple came over, and afterwards the man said to my husband that they're not coming to our house anymore because I will corrupt his wife. We had a student coming to stay with us for a few weeks from interstate, and my son said to him: 'My mother is a feminist, you'll be living in a feminist household. Don't expect her to do things for you'.

AGNES: It's great that your son just takes it for granted.

HELEN: Yes, and my husband too. Perhaps I didn't mention it before because to me it's just normal. But my brother pointed it out to me. He said: 'I couldn't live like that. What's a wife for?' So I'm reminded that in other households things don't happen the way they do in ours.

AGNES: Yes, when we talked about expectations I only talked about personal stuff. I'm so used to the fact that everybody in my house does their own washing and ironing. And we're on a roster system for cleaning up. I just forget that's not typical.

GLORIA: Well, you were saying something about the age. My husband is almost seventy. It says a lot for him that he now has a working wife, and he tries to do a lot of things he's never done before. I have some gay friends, and we've had to talk about it . . . he's taken a long time to come to terms with it, but he accepts it. For a man of his years . . . he does try.

HELEN: That's wonderful, and it can't be easy.

AGNES: Yes, even though everyone does their own washing, there are still things that I haven't been able to change within *myself*. So if I was seventy years old and there was nothing in it for me . . .

HELEN: So, he's still learning things, even at his age. But if you were a different woman perhaps he wouldn't.

GLORIA: He wouldn't be able to accept a lot of things that he does now. I'm always talking to him and explaining things. And I realise he's also given back a lot of his own feelings and fears. He feels safe to talk with me about them but he wouldn't tell anybody else. So there is a lot more communication in this relationship.

RITA: That's something I miss a lot. I miss having lots of friends, people I can ring up, people I can go and see. Not that there was much of that once I started living with my partner, even before we moved. But I had quite a few visitors, both males and females, when I was living by myself. And I would really . . . anybody who comes to my house for a cup of coffee or to stay overnight would be treated like royalty.

Then the conversation turned to relationships with other women; to whether the importance of strong relationships with women had increased or diminished since those days in the CR group. They had all considered contact with each other to be essential. Had they outgrown the desire for that sort of intense relationship with women friends or had that early experience established a life-long precedent?

GLORIA: The nature of my relationships with women has changed as a result of those CR days. Generally I'm more trusting of women, and I'm more honest with them. And I have one very carefully chosen best friend who I can tell anything to.

AGNES: Do you mean that you trust women now more than you used to, or more than you trust men?

GLORIA: Oh, both. I feel very comfortable with telling them my feelings, and they seem to respond better than I think men would. I'm amazed at what happens when I open up and let another woman know how I feel. Once I would have been too scared, in case she put me down, but I get such a good response. And the more I show them how I feel, the more they do the same.

AGNES: I tend to spend my time mostly with women. Also, the people I know who are in positions of some power and influence tend to be women. That may be just in the area I work in, but nevertheless, it's really nice to see women heading things.

HELEN: I'm at an age when sex is not as important anymore. So purely based on needs for friendship and working relationships, I could live without men. I feel so comfortable with women that I seek them out. And I find that I can't just have one friend. I have to have different friends for different purposes . . . networks, you know . . . so all my needs are covered. And I'm not possessive about women friends . . . I may not see them for months and then we pick up as though we never stopped.

RITA: One of my best friends is about fifteen years older than me. She does a lot of artistic things. She's a very open person . . . very outspoken too. So I can get a lot out of her. I suppose I use her a lot, because she can respond if I tell her how I feel about something to do with my partner, whereas if I tried to explain to *him* how I feel about what he's done or said, there's nowhere near that type of understanding.

But for some reason I haven't developed any really strong relationships with other women. I've sort of lost touch with old friends. As a matter of fact, a couple of weeks ago I rang two women I haven't seen for years. I had a long conversation with both of them, and said: 'Be sure to stay in touch'. But I haven't heard from either of them since. I think they've developed in different ways from me . . . if I've developed. They've had different experiences.

HELEN: Are you interested in going to any of the womens' events that come up every now and then?

RITA: Oh, yes. If I had someone to go with. I probably wouldn't go by myself. But, I did go to something. It was a series of women's performances that went over a whole weekend.

HELEN: I often do that. If there's a workshop on the weekend about health or IVF, or anything like that, I often go.

RITA: I'd go to something if I was part of it . . . getting to be part of it is the hard thing. You know, unless I sort of take the initial step and say: 'My name is Rita and I want to become part of this' it doesn't happen.

GLORIA: No, I always say I'm going to but I never get there. *(Laughs.)* Hearing you talk. I realise I've been lazy. I'm interested but I don't make the effort. I keep saying I'll do things like that when I retire.

HELEN: Well, I find it very enjoyable. I've made lots of acquaintances with women which I've followed up, and I like the way women talk. They're practical. Women say things that I can relate to. I really get great joy out of seeing women scientists talking about issues, and being very careful about looking at consequences . . . like Renate Klein on the IVF program. I think we have got to take control of these things for ourselves. We have to look at them from our perspective, not always from a male perspective.

Everyone agreed on the benefits of taking part in activities organised for and by women. Then Gloria picked up the questionnaire which had been circulated, and pointed to the section on 'Authority Figures', commenting that she now saw them as people who work for her benefit rather than as people who could look down on her. It is probably significant that this reference to authority figures led to a discussion on how the women felt about men, in general as distinct from those men with whom they were living.

HELEN: Well, after fifty years I've come to the conclusion that a lot goes into keeping up the myth that men are big and strong. This is true whether you're talking about a little boy or the President of the U.S.A. If I have to deal with men in business, I just ignore the image they try to put across.

GLORIA: I know this is a generalisation, but in my experience I have found that men are much weaker, emotionally, than women. I mentioned before that there had been a crisis in our family recently. Well, the men just went to water, and the women did what had to be done.

HELEN: I've had the same experience. But I don't mean to say that I'm contemptuous of men . . . in fact it makes them seem more human. I just have to chuckle when I think of all these years that I was conned into thinking they were special people . . . more intelligent, tougher emotionally . . . when the truth is that they're just as vulnerable as I am. Now, if a man tries to bully me, I just think 'blow on it' . . . and that doesn't show much respect.

GLORIA: Well, I wouldn't say I have no respect for men. I'm beginning to accept that that's the way they are, and they've been conditioned too. They have to put on this big brave façade and inside they're shaking like a jelly, and I feel sorry for them. We can show our emotions and then go ahead and do what has to be done, whereas a man has to show a stiff upper lip . . . that's what men like my husband have been taught . . . and inside they're terrified.

HELEN: Yes, maybe respect is the wrong word. They're sad, really. Let's just say they don't have the same effect on me that they used to have.

GLORIA: I know in my marriage I'm the dominant personality. I make all the decisions to the point where, at times, I think he is not sharing enough of the responsibilities. Which is really a reversal of what a lot of people imagine.

Helen and Gloria had been speaking of strength in emotional and intellectual terms. Here Rita discussed strength in terms of physical confidence, and of how men accept that confidence as a birthright.

RITA: Just recently I've become acquainted with some transsexuals. We've met one in particular who's taken the big plunge and had an operation. And she's commented to us several times about the way men treat women, now that she's become aware of it. She was saying her strength's gone now. She used to be able to walk anywhere, go anywhere, and now she can't.

GLORIA: It's amazing. We just grow up taking those restrictions for granted. Think how powerful the sense of threat must be. I mean, if a man who has always felt safe out there takes on the appearance of a women and suddenly feels . . . fear . . .

They return to attitudes towards men.

RITA: How do I feel about men? *(Rita thinks for a minute, then makes a sound that is impossible to reproduce, and the group laughs appreciatively.)* Yeah, I'm disappointed mainly. Just disappointed.

AGNES: I've been told that I'm fairly scary to some men . . . I guess because my feminism is up front in my working life and my social life too. So I've come to think of myself as some kind of test for a man. If he likes me then he must be okay because I don't make any concessions. I'm reasonably friendly I think, but I don't bat my eyelashes anymore and I don't keep my mouth shut anymore.

I like the men who like me. Some of my best friends are men. *(The women laugh in agreement.)* But I agree with you about the weaknesses, and I think some of the greatest casualties of the last two decades have been the men who are my age and bewildered by everything that's happened to male and female roles in those twenty years.

RITA: The image of the '80s male that the media put out was totally different to my experience of reality. I mean in my own close personal relationships. Mind you, there haven't been all that many . . . not enough for me really to analyse it. But the '80s image was that men had become a whole lot more sensitive. You know, television programs all through the decade were showing men crying . . . a *lot*. And that was supposed to really mean something. But I don't know. If they still have the same duties and the same responsibilities, and if they still think control belongs with them, then they haven't changed.

AGNES: I read something about some kind of physiological differences in men and women . . . in their ability to deal with conflict. This study said that there's actually a change that takes place in men when the point is reached in a conflict where they have to take some action. And they would actually rather avoid this situation. If they *can't* they'll fight sooner than a woman will, but their first preference is to *avoid*. That was presented as one explanation for why men won't talk when there's an argument. They'd rather do anything. And according to this article, that's something that comes from deep inside them. Of course, if that's the case, we're all stuffed anyway. *(Everyone laughs.)*

GLORIA: You mean they'll fight physically, but only if they can't get out of doing anything at all?

AGNES: Yes, and I mean . . . that's okay in an armadillo, but not in your *men*.

RITA: If that's the case, what hope is there? One of the political theories is that there could be complete understanding all over the world, brought about through communication and co-operation.

AGNES: Maybe there's some hope in the fact that you can be trained to go beyond your initial response to things, if you realise that it handicaps you.

Finally the women discussed how they felt about themselves. In many ways the conversation up to this point was about just that . . . but now they were asked to express what they thought about this stage in their lives and how their perspective on various issues had changed as they had grown older.

HELEN: I think I'm great!

GLORIA: You took the words right out of my mouth. Yes, when you were talking about Renate Klein, I thought about medical research, and the huge impact it's had on society, and so much of it is especially relevant for women. Women are required to know so much more. In our age group there's menopause and the changing attitudes to it. There's so much going on. I reckon we're in the best stage of our lives, we have our children out of the way . . . we can be so useful and so productive in our fifties.

HELEN: Yes, and up till now it was an age group that wasn't politically powerful, but I think we are changing. We're ageing, but we're feeling good and strong, and it makes us interested in *doing* things.

GLORIA: Yes, I've been thinking how good I feel lately. There's so much I can do now that I don't have to look after anybody. I *don't* feel old, and I *don't* feel tired, and I'm more confident.

HELEN: I'm comfortable, I'm happy . . . I don't even care anymore that my thighs are a bit fat. There are a lot of things that used to worry me when I was younger that I don't care about anymore. I feel fine. I accept myself.

GLORIA: Exactly. I wonder if it *is* our age. I think, *This is how I am and that's it.*

AGNES: Are we supposed to say how the women's movement has affected all this? Because I think there are too many influences to pin it down to that.

HELEN: No, I think it's a lot of things. It's maturing, it's experience. It's personal and historical. So you don't really know what came from what. It's more than just the women's movement though.

AGNES: I used to think, as a younger woman, that older women felt worse about themselves as they aged. Maybe they did, but I don't.

GLORIA: I don't either. I feel younger than I did twenty years ago. Life's a challenge. I'm careful about my health. When I got to the point that I didn't like what I saw in the mirror, I stopped looking in the mirror. That's it . . . And I also believe that people accept you for your personality and who you are instead of what you look like.

AGNES: I heard the actress Sally Fields interviewed on television the other day. Somebody in the audience commented on how good she looked, as though it was really surprising at her age. And she said: 'This is the way forty-two looks these days'. And it's true.

HELEN: Yes, the time is gone when you're old at thirty. The media is full of women who are forty and fifty. You don't hear the word 'matron' any more. It's 'mature woman' or 'successful woman' or 'business woman'. It's a different attitude.

RITA: I wonder what they call men in hospital who are matrons.

GLORIA: I think they call them matrons.

RITA: I was just thinking. My partner likes to go to nudist beaches. He prefers them to ordinary ones. I really don't care, although I don't like the thought of him insisting on the nudist beach anymore than I would like it the other way round. That kind of thing bothers me a bit.

HELEN: Don't you feel comfortable when you're there? What worries you about it?

RITA: I feel comfortable . . . I don't know . . . I really can't bring myself to believe that all the people who go along to nudist beaches are going there solely for the freedom of not having to wear bathers. *(Murmurs of agreement.)*

GLORIA: No, but if that's why you go there that's all you have to worry about.

RITA: I go because my partner likes to go. *(Rita laughs, but without humour.)*

HELEN: So what are you saying?

RITA: *(She takes a few minutes to answer.)* Well, I haven't achieved anything. Not that I ever dreamed of achieving anything specific. I guess I just hoped that one day I would achieve, and then I would feel like I owned myself. Like I was totally in possession of myself . . . full of self-confidence. Self-awareness. That's it, self-awareness. And I don't really think I can get there.

See, I stopped teaching . . . for a number of reasons . . . and the only thing I do is a bit of acting occasionally. But it's not a full time job by any means. Maybe if I'd stuck with teaching . . . maybe if I'd said okay, that's what I am — a teacher . . .

AGNES: Did you like teaching?

RITA: Not much. But I put it down mostly to the fact that I was an emergency teacher, and that's soul destroying. You don't establish any relationship with the children. You have no real authority. The only reason you do it is for the money.

GLORIA: But when you say you haven't achieved anything . . . does that determine how you see yourself, or can you imagine the day when you just accept yourself.

AGNES: . . . which is an achievement in itself.

RITA: No. I don't know. I feel I do nothing. I feel like a slug. I could have pushed harder, sold myself more. I probably could have got a job with my B.A. and ended up an executive, but then I'm not business-orientated either.

GLORIA: I love teaching but I got started too late. I don't like to admit it, but I think I let people discourage me: my family, my parents, my children, my husband. They were comfortable with me being a housewife, a mother. They didn't want to know about me as an individual. So I look back and I'm a little angry about that but it was my own fault. I can't blame anybody else really for my not pursuing what I wanted to achieve. I'm certainly happy with all that I *have* achieved.

HELEN: I don't think I link my job with my self-esteem so much. I think I'd feel just as good about myself if I worked in a shop. Perhaps that's a thing about ageing too. Because there comes a time when you look in the mirror and you see your wrinkles, and it's very important, when you get to that stage, to have sorted out how you feel about yourself.

GLORIA: Yes, I'm thinking about resigning. Most teachers my age are in administrative positions. I go home and I fall asleep for half an hour before I eat my dinner because I'm so tired. I have no social life. I have to decide whether the intellectual stimulation is worth the physical exhaustion, and at the moment it's very finely balanced.

HELEN: But if you got out of it, you wouldn't feel bad about yourself?

GLORIA: No, when I finally make that decision, I've got so much I want to do . . . waiting for me.

AGNES: Well, I still think my self-esteem is related to working. But earlier this year I wanted to change jobs, and I've been doing the one thing for so long that I wasn't sure I could do anything else. Anyway, I applied for this job which was totally different. It involved some pretty high level organisation. And you know what made me think I could do it? The fact that I'd run a home and a family for years. I realised that took a lot of administrative skill. In the end, I got the job. But even if I hadn't, being forced to look at all the things I do well was a good thing.

HELEN: Right. When Rita said she didn't feel she'd achieved anything . . . I think she needs to sit down and say: 'Okay, I brought up two children and I managed a household'. This is where we often undervalue ourselves.

Rita considered this, and admitted that she had actually accomplished things, but she was dissatisfied because all those accomplishments belonged to the past. Her real problem was not that she had never done anything of value, but that she wasn't doing anything now.

AGNES: It sounds like there's a big empty space in you that's waiting to get filled.

RITA: Yes, yes!

GLORIA: And it probably will get filled. Don't worry, you have plenty of time left. And it's good that you don't feel like you've achieved everything you want, because you won't rest on your laurels. You've got so many more years ahead of you than Helen and I. Now that I look back, and because I'm really at the end of my working career, there's not much time left for me, I really wish I had pushed it further.

HELEN: Yes, you very quickly get your act together when you know you're running out of time. When you look at the ads for jobs they say: 'Mature person is required, age from 30 to 45'. I believe in the proposed changes to the Anti-discrimination Act they're going to make that against the law.

GLORIA: I actually lied on my last job application; I knocked four years off my age. But isn't it a shame that all that experience and maturity don't count for more?

HELEN: Yes, and all the new confidence that comes when you get past a certain age. And being able to devote yourself to the job instead of the children or the husband or the dog or your boyfriend.

This grievance against ageism in the workforce led to a discussion about bosses in particular, and then other authority figures. A lot was said about the phenomenon of status dividing women.

HELEN: As far as employers are concerned, I won't let myself be intimidated anymore. But I don't expect to be treated any differently by a woman boss just because we're both women. Some of them only survive by acting like men.

AGNES: Actually, nothing scares me more than some of these high-powered shoulder-padded women.

GLORIA: When I went back to study, I always felt that the women tutors were much harder on me and the other mature-age students, who were mostly women than the male tutors. The men tended to be more helpful. But the women marked us harder, and gave us less help than they did the younger students. I don't know why. We were older than most of the women tutors, and perhaps they were a bit scared of us, because they knew we'd had more experience.

RITA: Well, the year I did my Dip. Ed. my women tutors were really good to me. It was a bad period in my life. I was going through my divorce, and I thought I was going insane, I really did. The women were very supportive. They understood, and it helped me a lot.

The discussion moved on to include other people in positions of some power. Gloria repeated that she now saw all teachers, doctors, bankers, etc. as being there to assist her, which marked a major shift in her thinking. The other women agreed that they now felt personally powerful, and in control of situations, although Agnes had a qualifying comment to make about that.

AGNES: I have to say that some of that confidence has to do with financial security. I remember being absolutely humiliated by a bank manager a few years ago, when all that was going into my account was a pension check. I got overdrawn once, by about seven dollars, and he called me into his office but he left the door open, and everybody in the bank could hear him talking to me like I was a stupid, naughty girl. I just felt completely at his mercy, and he treated me as though I was worthless. It showed me how degrading poverty is.

HELEN: Yes, and it's mostly women in that category. The supporting parent.

GLORIA: And women who aren't educated, who don't know their rights, who have no money. I really believe financial independence as an individual is very important. I used to think emotional independence was more important. Now, I don't know whether it's because I'm older, I see things differently.

When I was first working, I never saw money as mine, but as ours. It went on food and things, and it was making our life much easier, but it wasn't acknowledged. Now suddenly I see it as mine. I'm earning it. I don't know why it has become so important. Is it because I'm getting older and my health may not always be good? I put what I earn in a separate account, in my own name where nobody can touch it. As an individual I made a decision, not as a couple. It's part of me maturing as a woman.

AGNES: Your whole sense of yourself goes when you don't have any money. I wasn't uneducated. And I came from a background where people expected — not servility, but service. And still, I allowed myself to be belittled by that bank manager. And I thought, if being broke could do that to me, what must it be like for women who haven't ever had any of those other advantages. *(Pause.)* I can't get over the fact that I let that man get away with it.

GLORIA: Yes, I remember those times too. They were bad. People behind counters acting superior. When somebody's down already, there's always somebody willing to kick them a bit lower.

RITA: I've never really had to go to bank managers. If we needed money from a bank it was always my husband who went to ask. Landlords used to make me feel a bit uncomfortable.

This issue of inequality is something I've worked on. Never, no matter who it is or what sort of a position the other person holds . . . never feel inferior. I used to feel that way with lots of people, just because of something in me. I think the CR group was probably a bit of a catalyst for working on that, but all the other experiences I've had have added to my determination.

AGNES: Well, when it comes to doctors, I'm ashamed to admit that I'm really slack. I don't very often have to see one, and when I do I'm grateful to anyone who makes whatever's wrong stop. I feel really guilty around Helen, because she gets a degree in chemistry every time she has a prescription filled.

My relationships with doctors have changed in the same way as my relationships with other people. I don't let anybody push me around anymore. But I'm not informed. I don't do private study on it. I'm basically conservative where medicine is concerned — *mea culpa*. But I do listen to other women.

The others laugh at Agnes's confession. At this point, as if to emphasise the value of women as experts, and incidentally recalling the old consciousness-raising ethic of sharing information, a long, fascinating symptom-swapping session on menopause and other manifestations of middle age took place.

GLORIA: I shop around until I find a doctor that will talk to me. If I'm not happy with one, I let them know, or I change, whereas years ago if I wasn't happy with something I just let it go. I put up with all those paternalistic attitudes because he was a specialist. I didn't demand explanations for things.

HELEN: I've decided that unless the doctor is willing to go into something . . . treatment, side-effects . . . with me completely beforehand, I'll walk out. I asked a very well-respected woman doctor for more information about some pills and she said: 'Don't worry about that'. So I said: 'Hang on. Yes, I do worry about that'.' And you know, she got quite antagonistic. But I insisted. It's my body and there's a doctor around every corner nowadays. I think all the feminist readings, and the articles in the newspapers, made me and other women start to be aware.

RITA: I was just thinking that I wish I hadn't had the sterilisation operation.

HELEN: What do you mean?

RITA: I just think I did it out of a sociological duty . . . I'd had two children and figured the world had enough people. I was very idealistic.

AGNES: I remember . . . you sort of had some misgivings at the time, didn't you?

RITA: Well, any that I may have had I pushed aside. *(Pause.)* I put them second to my husband and the children, our marriage, peer group, world population, politics . . . I don't think I ever really considered how I felt.

As a matter of fact, after a few years I became so incensed about the tubal ligation that I had a reversal. I was told at the time it had a fifty percent chance of being successful so I went on the pill for a while. But then I went off it and nothing happened, so I figured I couldn't get pregnant after all. Then, about four years ago, I discovered that I *was*. So I told my partner and he didn't like it at all. He doesn't want to share me with anyone . . . my kids, his own kids . . . you know, my friends, anyone. So . . . I had an abortion.

HELEN: Didn't anybody counsel you? That was really bad.

RITA: Well, the woman who counselled me tried really hard to sound like her heart was in it, but I could tell it was just a job to her. She was saying that single mothers can manage quite well these days . . . but then, my partner was there too, and I guess I was more concerned about what his opinion was.

HELEN: Didn't you think, *What about me, don't I have anything to say about it?* What if you'd kept the baby?

RITA: I don't know what he would have done if I'd wanted the child so bad that I'd said: 'I'll go off and have it by myself'. I don't know if, after that, when he'd cooled down, he would have rung me up and said: 'Come on, look, it's my responsibility. I'll pay for it, and I'll take care of you and the baby'.

AGNES: Did he realise everything you'd been through?

RITA: Yeah, yeah I told him.

GLORIA: When you found out you were pregnant what were your first feelings?

RITA: What's he going to think?

GLORIA: Wasn't there any joy?

RITA: Yes, for me.

HELEN: Doesn't that affect your relationship now? Doesn't it come out when you're angry . . . that he prevented you from having a child?

RITA: *(Long pause.)* Yeah . . . it's difficult.

HELEN: Did you ever consider having it by yourself? I mean, it was really in your hands to say whether you wanted an abortion or not.

RITA: Well, no, I guess I just . . . I've always been influenced by what those close to me say. My mother was saying: 'Oh, you don't want to have another child'.

AGNES: But, after the lengths you went to . . . it was such a big thing to have an operation to reverse the tubal ligation . . .

HELEN: . . . and then to have an abortion . . . especially if you really wanted the child? It just makes me wonder how much of your life is your own.

The atmosphere in the room was very tense at this point. The other women were clearly shocked and distressed by Rita's revelations. She in turn seemed bewildered by the intensity of their reaction and said she felt she had been placed on the defensive.

AGNES: I think our response is just in proportion to what you went through. It's like you've let yourself be mutilated, not once, but several times.

RITA: Yeah, I don't know. *(Pause.)* My family . . . they sort of ganged up on me.

AGNES: But the bit you're leaving out is how *you* felt.

RITA: Well, at the time I thought it would be great if I could have the baby, and if my partner would be really happy about it, and we could get a big house, and . . . but then I thought that was just moving back into the situation I was in before, when I was married. And I thought, *What progress is that?*

If I'd had kind of guy who would have wanted to be present at the birth . . . involved with the baby . . . you know . . . then it would have been different and I would have gone ahead with it. But there were so many problems lined up in front of me, including not having any emotional help.

Rita's story elicited sadness and anger, questions and advice. The discussion dealt with women breaking free of outside influences over their bodies and their lives, but acknowledged how difficult this is in reality. They talked about how many women had been forced to choose between the man they loved and the child they might have loved.

GLORIA: When I think back over my life, I realise some of the things doctors have done to me. When I had my tubes tied I wasn't told to expect heavier periods. For a few months I was virtually confined to my bed for the first day. It became an illness whereas I'd never been sick before. I should have been told about that.

When I complained about it the doctor said why didn't I just have a hysterectomy. That would solve the problem. Then he gave me a referral to a specialist, which I opened and read. It said that I was quite neurotic about a hysterectomy so they'd have to do something else for these heavy periods. I was neurotic! I had a healthy womb and I wasn't going to have any parts of it removed. I should have said to him: 'You've got two testicles and you only need one. Perhaps we could take out one of your testicles'.

Interview 2: 28 March 1990
Bernadette, Sue, Helen, Jane, Sophia and Agnes

For this interview we met at Bernadette's house. Gloria and Rose were not able to get there, but the others contributed to a lively, rambling discussion before, during and after dinner. Transcribing the tapes of this session involved listening to a good deal of crockery-rattling, cutlery-scraping and glass-clinking.

Before we could begin we needed to tell the women that Rita had pulled out of the project. Rather than presume to explain her reasons for this we passed on her invitation for them to contact her directly.

On this night the topic was again the women's relationships with the important people in their lives, their attitudes towards themselves, and how if at all these had altered over the years. Of course, we were particularly interested in what part their experiences in the CR group, and the wider movement, played in their expectations of themselves and others. Jane began by echoing some of the sentiments she had expressed in an earlier interview.

JANE: The women's movement changed my life dramatically, in all ways, but I don't know whether it made me a better person to live with. I would say it taught me to be more selfish, perhaps . . . more demanding . . . and to be comfortable about that.

The first time I got married it was just because that was what you were supposed to do. The second time I got married was for entirely different reasons, and none of them to do with wanting to be married. It was a financial thing. If it hadn't been for that I probably wouldn't have got married.

SUE: Would you still be with him if you weren't married?

JANE: I don't know. There were times when I wanted to break free. Does marriage keep you there? I don't know. I doubt it, because I don't actually *feel* married. I think you just stay long enough, and you get to an age where the . . . wanting to be free . . . just fades away.

HELEN: Also when you live with somebody long enough and you sort of set your own pattern . . . you're probably more likely to stay. The second time around you make sure you get yourself that

freedom. The first time you think you've got to be always together
. . . that this makes a marriage happy.

SUE: I'm not married. If I married anybody it would be my present partner. He's a difficult man . . . very volatile . . . hard to get on with, but fascinating. Terrific and generous . . . and selfish. Sometimes he has a flash of being a macho man. That irritates me.

We've been together coming up to three years now. There are days when I think being on my own would be bliss. I just want to lie on my bed alone and look out the window and see the rain . . . solitude . . . But then I really don't want to be without him. He generally gets his own way and I hate him for that. I hate myself for letting him get his own way. We play these little power games. When he has these flashes of ill temper I tell him: 'I can live without you, don't worry'. But I don't want to. I want this relationship to work.

He's a very sexual person. Anything to do with sex is natural and easy with him. Talking about sex is easy. It's different from how it was with my husband.

BERNADETTE: What about talking about other things?

SUE: Oh, any talking's easy. He lets me into his head. In fact I probably have to do more listening than I want to sometimes. Of course I'm always more of a listener. A lot of yelling though. I never did that with my husband. I would never do it in front of the kids. In my first marriage it was one of those controlled things. We only argued under the bed covers. That's what my mum and dad did.

JANE: I've been married for a long time now, over ten years. And we have conversations, not about anything particularly world shattering. But communication's not really a problem.

SUE: Actually, I think Jane's biggest problem with her husband is the same as mine with my partner: the kids. Having kids that aren't your partner's causes more tension than anything. If the kids weren't around it would be absolute bliss.

JANE: Yeah, that's the hardest part of the relationship. And it isn't the mother's fault. There's all the haranguing and hassling about trivial things, and you're the one who is sort of in the middle all the time. It's a horrible situation to be in.

Last year I really was planning to leave. I just couldn't hack the conflict that was going on. I felt torn, and I thought, *I don't need this*. I just assumed that I'd go and take my daughter with me. She was seventeen.

But the interesting thing is . . . *(chuckles)* . . . she left *me* instead! Because she couldn't stand the demands I was putting on her. Like what time she was going to be home, that sort of thing. So . . . you know . . . you waste so much energy. I could have left with her, and then five minutes later she would have been gone.

I don't know whether fathers of kids act any differently from stepfathers; whether the conflict is still there, where they pull one way and mother pulls the other way.

AGNES: I wish I could be sure that the father of my children will have that kind of bond with them that means no matter how much they yell at each other, the kids would always know . . . and the father would know . . . that they just have to love each other. The way the kids and *I* know it about each other.

No argument can make the slightest difference to this . . . this thing between us that can't be touched. It's why the fights with stepfathers aren't okay . . . because they don't have that relationship. But when it goes right down to it, I don't know if fathers do either.

JANE: I don't know if men are really able to respond to kids in the way that women do. The things they do when their relationships split suggest they can't. Like not keeping up maintenance. It doesn't seem to hurt them if their kids are deprived, as long as they pay the woman back, whereas the mother always wants the kids to have the things they need.

BERNADETTE: I do know some men who have really close relationships with their children. My husband was equally determined to have my son.

HELEN: But was that determination just part of a power game?

BERNADETTE: No, he was genuinely bonded to my son. And of course, he was into all that . . . he delivered four babies for his other partner, without a doctor present.

This comment was greeted with surprise, and something that sounded suspiciously like sexist amusement. Then the issue of equality within relationships was taken up. Interestingly, each of the women who responded did so in terms of economics.

JANE: Financially I am in the superior position. So I think this probably makes a big difference in regard to equality. There can't be any argument about it. If it's an issue, it's only one for *him*. It's a powerful thing to be the breadwinner, or financially independent . . . *(pause)* . . . But does that mean that until all women are on equal pay they'll never be equal?

SOPHIA: That's self-evident, really.

SUE: Then your state of mind doesn't make any difference, does it? I *feel* equal but when we talk about wage-earners . . . what does that make me?

JANE: Men have always defined the power in terms of their capacity to earn money. So it's hard for us not to see it in that way.

SOPHIA: The fact is that money is so important in society it even defines the way you value yourself. As much as we insist that our capacity to draw income has nothing to do with what we believe we're worth . . . money equals status. I mean . . . this is the world we live in.

AGNES: I think it's different if you don't share incomes. I don't make as much money as my partner, but it's irrelevant because I decide how to spend mine. He doesn't pay my bills.

Things have changed in subtle ways over the years. There's nothing like a property settlement to make you want to keep things separate the next time. So at first he lived in my house and paid board. He doesn't pay any more, but he does other things; we've worked out a material trade. And we share expenses like groceries and utilities. We take turns shouting each other to movies and plays and dinners.

SOPHIA: So that arrangement gives you equal power within the relationship.

AGNES: Yes, my discretionary income just doesn't get discussed with him, or his with me. If I decided to do something really extravagant I wouldn't have to explain it to him. To me that's really important.

After the women traded accounts of their efforts to achieve financial autonomy within their relationships, Sophia returned to the question of expectations of one's self. She revealed how psychoanalysis had given her valuable insights into choices she made during her twenties and thirties.

SOPHIA: I think the women's movement kept me away from men, from heterosexual relationships, by reinforcing all the negative feelings I'd had about female images when I was a girl. I didn't want to grow up to be the European mamma; I didn't want the life my mother had. Pursuing a career and being involved in political issues was really all about my need to break from my peasant past.

The break was made easier when my father died. I took over the leadership role in the family and developed a lot of masculine characteristics. The women's movement was convenient because it confirmed that what I was doing was correct; having the strength and the courage to pursue an education rather than staying at home.

Between 1972 and 1982 there were no men in my life, and after that I had a history of relationships with men who were all much younger than me. My psychiatrist says that I was basically catching up with what I'd missed in my twenties. And I can proudly announce that I've finally caught up. *(Everyone laughs.)* It's wonderful because I'm starting to have relationships with men who are older than me, and I've started to find my femininity. But I still have regrets about losing touch with it during my period in the movement. I realise that's a very controversial thing to say. It's been a very big shock for me to realise it.

I used to feel that men had it all over us when it came to qualities I admired. I don't think I saw any traits in womanhood that I wanted to express, because I identified them with weakness and passivity and I saw myself as a person of strength and action.

I'm not blaming the movement, though obviously my anger was often fed by the other women. We contributed to each other's sense of injustice. But there was more than just the anger.

I lost touch with the soft part of me; the person who really didn't want to lead all the time. The person who *did* want a shoulder to lean on. Somehow that seemed to represent the worst characteristics of womanhood. So, I shunted it all away and worked hard at everything that was the opposite. Everything that said: 'I'm here. These are my opinions. These are my decisions. I'll do it. You're irrelevant. You're male. Here let me show you. I'll go and organise the world. I don't need you'. That certainly paid off enormously in terms of career, but I paid a personal price for it. I made the classic mistake of ignoring the positive virtues of women. It was a cruel wound that I inflicted on myself.

AGNES: That's really interesting. I used to find a paradox in the big meetings where the central figures in the movement seemed to be caricatures of men. Why wasn't a women's movement about celebrating women, not disguising them?

BERNADETTE: I remember meetings where it was obvious that one group of influential women didn't take us seriously because we related to men.

SOPHIA: I don't want to do what I've heard some other feminists do, which is to blame what happened to me on those women, or that era, or the organisation. You see, I think there was always that real splitting in me . . . I got involved with the lesbian women at a personal level, but at the same time I still kept this link with this bunch of really ordinary, lovely women out in the suburbs . . . I had both those scenes. *(Here everyone laughs at the memory of Sophia having to defend herself for going to CR with housewives.)*

So there must have been something in me. It was like . . . the central thing . . . the politics . . . was about change. But what was happening out there in the suburbs was real life. People changing themselves. That was the 'personal is political' idea. That was the true definition of politics. But I had to feel that I was a . . . crusader . . . a legitimate part of an organised group that brought about concrete changes.

JANE: Maybe there was an element of that in coming to the CR group . . . you were trying to move all these bludgers out in the suburbs!

SOPHIA: I don't know. Did I come across like that?

AGNES: No. You weren't a missionary.

SOPHIA: It was a bit like a refuge. Like keeping contact with reality, because I kind of knew what was happening down at LaTrobe Street [Women's Centre] was . . . manufactured, you know. That it was a little laboratory where all these hot experiments were going on. And it was explosive . . . all exciting and dynamic!

At this point we stopped to refill coffee cups, and came back to the subject of intolerance. The general feeling was that rigid expectations of ourselves and others was at least as much the product of immaturity as of strident feminism.

There was at least a little pride mixed in with the laughter as the women discussed how they had learned to go with the flow.

SOPHIA: I accept people who have faults and weaknesses . . . and yes, I think I'm a lot more tolerant than I was in the years when I was going to the CR groups. I think I'm capable of embracing a lot more . . . damage. Damaged men, damaged women. And where in the past I might have argued with them or just moved away from them, now I say: 'Well, I'm disagreeing with you, but I recognise that you've been through your bad experiences . . .' I remain silent, or perhaps try to make a point differently.

HELEN: I think this is the kind of attitude that comes to you with maturity.

AGNES: It's a pity we have to spend so much time being young and big-mouthed.

SUE: Oh, yes. Except for meetings with the group, social situations back then were a total misery. I just spent ten years *arguing*. I alienated myself from everybody because of my feminist feelings. They couldn't say anything without me making an issue of it. When Jane was around it wasn't so difficult, but when I was out with my husband or his work mates it was terrible. The confrontations . . . I was probably ridiculous.

JANE: We know someone who's doing that now . . . she talks the way we would have fifteen years ago . . . and you find yourself cringing. She constantly interprets everything from a feminist perspective, no matter what anybody says. And she gets really emotional about it. And I can now see why we were so obnoxious. We were so *right*. We thought all we had to do was tell people and they'd see the light, but they kept bloody arguing with us!

SOPHIA: I was at a party recently and the word 'bitch' was used. And I was so shocked that I didn't say anything, just let it flow. But I thought to myself, *This guy has a twenty-two-year-old daughter. She'll pick him up on it some day. And if not, well it's her world.* I've moved on to other things.

Here Bernadette explains how the events of her life since the group disbanded have contributed to altered expectations, both of herself and others.

BERNADETTE: I don't know. I feel as if I have been all over the place since I broke up with my husband. I wasn't happy in the relationship. I was interested in the growth movement and that, together with the women's movement, showed me that you have to do things for yourself.

My involvement in the women's movement was based on my being a mother, in a way . . . I wanted to bring up daughters to have non-sexist ideas about their own future. I wanted to open up the possibilities for other role models. And I got a lot out of it. But a lot of the energy and drive came from my husband rather than me. He wanted me to be his equal. And perhaps that was a reasonable thing for him to want, but at the time I resisted it. After I had my baby he wanted me to work half the time so he'd only have to work half the time.

SOPHIA: That's amazing! He took women's liberation literally . . . in economic terms.

BERNADETTE: Perhaps I should have been more open to that, but I wasn't really. I was quite annoyed. *(Bernadette laughs, but she is clearly stifling another feeling.)* I'd put it more strongly than that but the tape's on. By the time the relationship broke up I didn't really know what had happened, except that I'd been screwed around. Then there was a real battle over our children. It was likely to tear them apart . . . so I ended up letting them go to him for a while.

Then I got involved in other sorts of relationships. I got involved with a group of anarchists. We lived in a house where we tried to completely break down sexual roles. But the bloke who was sort of head of the house had all these rules. *(The unintentional irony in this comment brought gales of laughter from the other women.)*

You had to be responsible for yourself and that related to sexual relationships as well. You could go to bed with anybody . . . you could all go to bed together if you wanted to . . . but you had to bring it out in the open. It was supposed to build up trust in your sexual relationships and then people would be able to be happy. But it's very hard. I don't think we're brought up to have really high esteem. So to let go of someone you love . . . let them go with somebody else . . . and feel that they love you just as much . . . it just doesn't work like that.

SOPHIA: I thought I was the big rebel!

BERNADETTE: Oh, I tried everything. But I didn't have the foundation to deal with it properly so it wasn't a constructive experience. I was naive and idealistic more than anything else. I guess it was a way of avoiding intimacy. I don't know if that was intentional, but I sort of suspect it was, because you do things to suit your own purposes even if you don't recognise it.

I see in retrospect that I didn't feel comfortable . . . and I still don't feel comfortable . . . being sexually involved with more than one person at a time. It's not a moral thing; it just never felt right for me. I find it very difficult to manage my energy in that way. It was a real disaster, and I didn't trust my ability to choose a partner. But underneath there was still a desire to have a family. When I did get involved with somebody else, it was a relationship where he supported me financially. So I had to please him because I was dependent on him. I gave up my own power and I wasn't being true to myself. Such a relationship can't really work in the long run but that one lasted for seven years.

When I returned to education and got a job things changed because I was economically independent. He was really quite a traditional man . . . and it caused a lot of problems when I stopped fitting into the role he thought was right for me. But I couldn't go back to it.

HELEN: You said the relationship started to change when you started earning some money.

BERNADETTE: Yes, the dynamics changed completely. He actually respected me when I was working. When I wasn't working he didn't respect me, which is a real contradiction, but for me it was very important. Now I don't need anyone else to provide for me. I have done it for myself. It's not really what I wanted to do, but I have been able to do it.

HELEN: It's interesting, how different you sound since the first interview we did together. You're definitely more positive.

BERNADETTE: Well, I'd just ended that relationship when you got the group together again, and I was quite low. I'll never be in that position again.

SOPHIA: I'm almost the opposite of you. I mean, having had a career, economic independence, achievement, success and my own home, now what I want is someone to share it with me. Career, money and all the rest of it is no longer part of my search.

BERNADETTE: I don't *want* to work. What I wanted to do was to have a family and be at home. But I guess you need to have both strings to your bow . . . *(pause)* . . . Life turned out to be a lot more complicated than I thought it was.

Here Bernadette responds to a question about the importance in her life of friendships with women.

I have friendships with women but I can't really be open with them. I could never tell them what has happened in my life. *(Bernadette considers for a moment.)* Actually I used to be a lot more open and I used to have what I thought were a lot more friends, women whom I could discuss anything with. Well, I don't have that anymore. I've closed up a lot. After all that happened to me I was in such despair that I lost my ability to communicate.

SUE: What about with your children?

BERNADETTE: Well, my expectations of them and myself have definitely changed. Before I had my first baby I thought that I was completely responsible for everything . . . I was a real smother-mother. I've changed with the others. I feel they are responsible for themselves. They came here, they have to survive. They have to do what's right for them.

SUE: Well, I always wanted a daughter but I ended up with two boys. I think they've got a reasonably good attitude towards women . . . but, who knows? I'd also like to think they aren't *racist*, but now and again something ghastly comes out of their mouths that they didn't get from me. So their attitude to women could be entirely different from what I expect or want. Only time will tell if my words and anguish and fights about the role of women will come through in their relationships with women.

As for my role in the house, I think there are still things they expect, but I don't really do much for them at all. I wash a bit and clean their room. I still play the mother role. My partner thinks I do much too much for them but compared to what other people do for their kids it's not much. They do a lot too.

Sophia, who has no children, and therefore no worries about what kind of a mother she has been, admits that something is missing now. While she says she won't go through the drama of hitting forty and saying: 'I've never done anything with my life', she is lonely and would like a partner.

SUE: Yes, that's how I felt. It's just that loneliness. I was quite happy alone but I remember coming home from work, just wanting to talk to somebody. There were just flashes. It didn't put me in a depression. I didn't really want somebody around all the time . . . just when I chose to have them. But there were times of distinct loneliness.

HELEN: I could never go from this marriage into another relationship, at least not straight away. If I ever left, it would be to live on my own. Living alone would be bliss after so many years of being constantly with somebody. But it's not really a reason to break up the marriage. I have been able to accommodate this need for solitude within the marriage. I deliberately make time for myself . . . to do things alone. If for some reason I couldn't do that anymore, it would probably change the situation. Maybe it would be the end.

JANE: Not so long ago there was this play on television. A man had just died, and his wife and his mistress were having afternoon tea together. One unforgettable line said that all their life married women actually look forward to their widowhood. That's when they start living. I can see the point.

HELEN: It's more complex than that. You have to consider it very carefully. You have to look at companionship in old age. Support if you become an invalid. It's very hard!

AGNES: Liking to be by myself and liking to be around my partner are two different issues for me. I've caught flack from people over the years for having a room of my own. I'm in a relationship with a man that I dearly love, but love isn't everything. I still want some privacy. Physical space. Mental space. And, you know, people think this proves I'm not really committed to the relationship.

HELEN: Yes. They actually ask you why you're married if you're not going to sleep together every night.

SOPHIA: What I'm thinking of for my next relationship is someone who already has his career, is financially established . . . he's had his family . . . and he's happy to just kind of go off and play with his . . . yacht . . . and he's willing to just be around from time to time. I could go on as I am and he could slot in. He could be this wonderful support person, but I wouldn't have to lose my independence.

There is a guy that I've recently been exploring a bit of a relationship with. He walked into my house, looked around, and said: 'You know, this is basically a place for one'. He couldn't see any space for himself there. And I said: 'I guess you're right. But I could always clean up the stuff in the study'.

The other women have found Sophia's thoughts on the ideal relationship highly amusing, but realise that she is making a serious point about the trade-off between independence and companionship.

It's like that when you come into it later on. What I need from a man now isn't necessarily highly sexual romantic love. It's really more of a mate thing, and not even that, because I've got all the women friends. It's just . . . the loneliness.

HELEN: And there are the week-ends, Easter, Christmas. It's nice to have somebody around the house then, and my women friends are usually with their family too on those days.

AGNES: You want Rent-a-Mate. For all your holiday needs.

SOPHIA: But I'd say your relationship with yourself has changed, because now you need less of the other person. And that's good. When you're younger, you pass that big responsibility for your happiness on to somebody else.

Now the discussion on changing relationships expanded to include those with employers, doctors, teachers, bankers, or as one of the women said: 'Everybody who ever made her feel terrible'. There was no attempt to restrict these comments to instances on which the CR group or women's movement had direct bearing. We realised there had been too many influences on their lives over the years for them to be able to attribute everything to the women's movement. But we were interested in looking further at shifts in power, and changes in attitudes to people who might be seen as authority figures.

SUE: I do remember when I went to get the big bankcard . . . at that time you could only get one if your husband signed for it. The manager said in order to approve my application he needed to know how much my husband earned. I said it had absolutely nothing to do with my husband. Then he asked what our house was worth. So I told him what half the house was worth . . . my half. That was all about standing up and being counted.

JANE: I had exactly the same experience. I still have that bankcard and it still has a $300 limit on it; in all those years they never offered to increase the amount.

HELEN: That's a reflection on income rather than gender. I don't think it's a deliberate act, but there is an underlying assumption that women don't climb the promotion and salary increase ladder.

Actually I had an experience at the bank only lately. I was trying to withdraw money under my own name from our business account, which is something I'm supposed to be able to do. I explained that I'm a partner of the firm and often withdraw money in my name. The clerk made a big fuss about it. I listened and then calmly asked him to either get me the manager or phone the bank's headquarters. He did check, and of course they gave him the O.K. A week later my husband went to the same bank to get money from the business account under his personal name and he got it without any question. So there is still discrimination, but the chap didn't intimidate me. I made my stand and I wouldn't have moved until I got my money.

JANE: Things have changed though. When I was sixteen I got a Myer's card in my name. When I got married it had to be cancelled and put in my husband's name. Then later when I remarried it had to be put in my second husband's name.

I had to operate on his card for years, until one day I thought, stuff it. All my life I've been on someone else's card. So I went to Myers and I said: 'Right, I want to take out a card'. I really expected a fight. Instead, I got the Myer's card in my name with cards for my two daughters and no problem's whatsoever. That would have been about three years ago.

I did get a small loan to buy a dishwasher, but fifteen years ago women couldn't get a loan for a house.

AGNES: What about with doctors? Do you know your rights with them?

SOPHIA: That's a big issue. I'm certainly much less likely to just accept what they're saying now. Recently I went through a very bad depression. My psychiatrist, a woman, wanted to prescribe drugs as well as therapy. I got two second opinions which agreed. But I just said: 'Sorry, I came through the 'seventies . . . and we question *everything*'. You remember the anti-psychiatry movement was big back then.

In the end I was able to resist the drugs. But in the past, I probably would have been overwhelmed by the opposition and done as I was told . . . accepted the existing power structure.

BERNADETTE: Actually when I went to hospital I was quite assertive, but the doctor still completely overrode what I said. So I realised you have to do more than say what you want, you have to fight for it. It's really difficult to get through, isn't it? When I did insist I got isolated. They thought I was a nut case. It created more problems.

SOPHIA: But it's better to go into all this questioning. You come out much more powerful, much more in control of the situation. And you can really see where traditional male authority is weak and you lose respect for it. It's important that you don't put the goals of the institution up on a pedestal.

BERNADETTE: You know they reckon that the birth of science was when they burnt the witches. They had to kill the female culture to bring in the male scientific culture. And all the wisdom and skill that women had was devalued . . . *(pauses)* . . . But I think if you do stick up for yourself you pay a certain price. You get disliked. It's like Jane said . . . you're more comfortable being yourself, but you don't know if you're nicer. You're not going along with people . . . and you lose that sense that you have when you're growing up, of being rewarded for being nice. The popularity thing.

HELEN: But then I always figure I'm not in a popularity contest. It's myself that really matters, not what people think of me.

BERNADETTE: Well, I always want people to like me. *(She laughs apologetically.)*

JANE: There is a certain satisfaction in *feeling* nice. I don't like to rock the boat particularly.

SOPHIA: Well, people's whole thrust in life is to minimise anxiety.

HELEN: But then there's a limit. I'm not going to sell out my principles just to be liked.

BERNADETTE: That's right, but it's hard. It's one of the things that we have to learn. I think women especially need to be acceptable. Even young girls . . . they do things to be nice, where boys often don't bother. So you have to sort of get over all that before you become assertive and comfortable with yourself. Or able to gauge if a situation is worth making a fuss about in order to get what you want.

AGNES: I hate it when people don't like me. And I hate that feeling that I get sometimes . . . like I'm alone with only my cantankerousness for company. I don't want to be the trouble maker. But it's so stupid that getting a doctor to explain something to you is considered not nice.

SUE: Do men get a better deal from doctors?

JANE: No, I don't think so.

BERNADETTE: Except that they don't chop their dicks off as easily as they cut out our wombs. And there are still a lot of women who are ignorant. They go along with what the doctor says. Have their operations. Have their bodies mutilated. I think Australia has the second highest incidence of Cesarean birth. Why aren't they asking questions? There is enough information around.

JANE: *(Drily)* When I was having my babies if the doctor said to me

I was going to have a Cesarean, I would have thought it was the best thing that could happen.

HELEN: But I get worried when they want to get my womb out. When I was about thirty-six . . . I was very much involved with the group at the time . . . I had a bit of trouble with my period and the specialist tried to convince me to have a hysterectomy. I just refused and never went back to him. No one ever mentioned hysterectomy to me again.

AGNES: I get confused when there's a traditional approach that actually seems to suit me better. Like going through the change of life . . . lots of my women friends say: 'Don't let them give you hormone therapy. Take Evening Primrose Oil drops'. So I take them and I still get hot flushes. Then I take hormones and I don't get hot flushes, and I think, fuck Evening Primrose Oil drops.

But things like that make me feel I'm letting the team down or something. Women I looked up to and respected were the ones who advised alternatives, and sometimes that meant stuff like using sea sponges for periods and risking toxic shock.

HELEN: When it comes right down to it, I say, stuff being ideologically sound if it makes me feel bad.

This session created much laughter. It seemed to provide more evidence that maturity had given the women a strong sense of what is appropriate for them as individuals. Now the conversation turned to their concerns about the young women of the next generation, and they swap a couple of stories about men who have trouble adjusting to the aftermath of women's consciousness raising.

BERNADETTE: I used to live in a flat next door to these girls. They had their boyfriends living with them, and they didn't know about any of the things that we've talked about . . . any of their options. They wanted to get married and have children and ignore economic independence. But there are some who are just the opposite;

they automatically know that they can have an abortion. They know how everything works and they use it.

AGNES: But I wonder if the ones who know they can have an abortion, realise what a short time it's been since it was illegal . . . and how it got changed. I wonder if they know the history.

Strictly speaking, abortion is still illegal in most parts of Australia. Victoria still has a British law from 1861 against 'unlawful abortion' on its statute books. But the 1969 ruling by Justice Menhennitt allows abortion in cases where a woman's physical or mental health is endangered.

SOPHIA: In my conversations with them I've observed an assumption that this is the way it's always been: that girls can have careers in any area, medicine, engineering, whatever they want.

JANE: I told my secretary, who's twenty-four, how dramatically the world has changed as a result of what went on in those years. She didn't realise that equal pay only came in 1972. When I was first married six o'clock closing was still in. Men went to the pubs and women led their own lives, with no job opportunities. And even the Pill was still in its infancy. She didn't know any of that, and she was quite stunned by it.

AGNES: Yes, I remember the women's magazines had something about the Pill in nearly every issue.

HELEN: And another thing was the second car! Most families had only one car and it was the husband's. A lot of women couldn't even drive. Or, if they had a second car, it was the mother and the kids who had the old bomb. And at parties the women were on one side of the room and the men on the other side.

BERNADETTE: Depending on what circle you move in, I think that still happens.

SUE: I know a young woman who's getting married shortly and her whole life revolves around that one thing. We had a conversation once and something came up about apartheid. She didn't know what it was. I think she thought it was a brand of coffee! I mean, it was amazing!

SOPHIA: Young women assume that jobs, education, money . . . and power are all theirs. But they have gone back to playing out the traditional role even more than we did. One of the glossy magazines ran a piece on an Australian business woman who is making heaps of money in the United States by flogging underwear to career women. They're paying astronomical prices for lacy satin gear to wear beneath those big shoulder pads. That message is really pushed very strongly now. You can have your career, but underneath it all you're still a woman. And it suits the economy too!

HELEN: Right. Women are in careers, but you look at who is in the top positions . . . in positions affecting policies and so on. That's still very much the domain of the males. You know why? Because the people hiring people for top positions are still mostly males. In art, in entertainment, those who count . . . who have influence . . . are still males.

SOPHIA: But that will change. Like in China, when the old men die. In another ten years we'll see a radical shift. In material terms women's positions have improved. But I think in terms of questioning sex roles women have actually gone backwards. And part of that is, as we always said, men have to change with us. We can't do it alone. And if I can't go on living life in isolation, if I'm complaining bitterly about my circumstances, then I have to compromise myself.

BERNADETTE: Haven't women always been the ones who did the compromising to make the marriage work? Men play golf at the week-end. Women look after the kids.

HELEN: But you know the older I get the less I compromise. I just can't be bothered.

SOPHIA: We had problems with the role that we'd had ascribed to us so we tried to change it, we fiddled around with the edges of it. But it's been different for men, because they don't see any problems with their role. They haven't done much re-jigging.

HELEN: Wouldn't you be reluctant to change anything if you were already on top?

AGNES: But has anyone else noticed all the incredibly damaged men in our age group? There seem to be a lot of them walking around saying: 'What happened? One minute she was happy, the next she burnt her bra'. And, you know . . . they still don't know what hit them.

SUE: They never recovered actually.

HELEN: No, and they are pathetic when they say: 'We were so happy till she walked out on me'. And years later they still can't comprehend why. They never saw anything wrong with the marriage.

AGNES: If you ask the woman, she'll say: 'I told him. I told him a *lot*. Harry, I said, this has got to stop or I'm out of here'. And five years after the divorce Harry is still saying: 'I never saw it coming. We were so happy. And then she took everything!'

SUE: A friend of mine said to her husband: 'If you're going to the pub tonight, I won't be here when you come back'. And she *wasn't* . . . When he came home he knew she was annoyed with him so he went to sleep in one of the other bedrooms. He got up the next morning and he thought 'something's wrong'. He checked and she was gone.

SOPHIA: I met this guy who decided to marry this woman on a whim, which was a stupid thing to do. He married in October last year and they split up in February when his best friend took off with her. So he was really shattered. He said to me that he never thought his wife would do that. I said: 'What about your best friend? It takes two'. But he's putting the blame on her. She destroyed the mateship.

AGNES: There's something else in that. I've had guys say to me: 'I never thought that my relationship with a woman was going to be the most important thing in the world. It's *one* of the most important, but it's not and never has been and never will be the thing which decides whether I'm happy or not happy'. That was quite a revelation, because I certainly grew up thinking that everything else depended on whether or not you had one central person in your life. I can remember as a teenager, having fights with boyfriends. I'd sit home by the phone being miserable, and he'd be off playing football.

HELEN: Does that come from women traditionally not having an identity of their own. I mean, first you're a daughter and then you're a wife, and then a mother.

AGNES: I don't know . . . I think it's all that Mills and Boon stuff.

SOPHIA: Some men just don't make having a relationship the most important thing in their life.

AGNES: But this doesn't make them bastards; that's my point. That's the sort of attitude I'd really like to aspire to. Men never had the magazines that said: 'Do this to make her notice you, do that to get close to her, do this to make her happy'. To my knowledge there isn't a single magazine that tells men how to hang on to their woman. I think that's really great.

BERNADETTE: I think it has a lot to do with women being mothers. The first few years after you have that baby, even if you want to be an individual it just doesn't work like that. It's a biological fact that we are a lot more pliable in how we respond to other people's needs. It goes really deep.

HELEN: Perhaps it also has something to do with our historical and social development. If we still had extended families we could bugger off and other members of the family could look after the children. Or if we were rich enough we could get a nanny.

SUE: That's right, there *is* a choice theoretically, but it's not a reality for most women.

This session ended with a long discussion on the question of feminist image and feminist backlash.

SOPHIA: What about the women who say: 'I used to be a feminist'.

BERNADETTE: It's funny, isn't it? You'd say you still have the same values, but they're modified a bit. They're humanist too. You see the other side of things.

HELEN: I'm still very much a feminist, but in my evening class there are two young women who are really radical feminists like the ones I used to know in the '70s. They look at everything we discuss from a feminist perspective. I can see their extremity, and they often antagonise the other students, especially the mature-age males. I listen to them and it takes me back fifteen years. They even dress the way militant feminists dressed when we first started going to the Women's Centre.

SOPHIA: Oh, women like that will always be around. It's good to know young ones are coming up.

AGNES: You know you said before that you don't want to criticise those women who didn't take our kind of feminism seriously. Well, I actually do resent them, but also, I'm sort of grateful to them because . . . they're the ones that put the challenge to me.

I can remember in those days . . . looking for the right *uniform* . . . for the right catchphrases, you know? So I could leave my traditional role and be a proper feminist. What I really wanted was the comfort of knowing the rules. *(Pause.)* In the end, there really was no cosy club for somebody like me to join. There were only my questions, and those women couldn't give me any answers I could use. I had to find the answers myself. The thing is, if those women had been any more welcoming to me, I probably would have settled for that. But they were so bigoted that it left me no choice but to stand on my own two feet. I had to stop looking for a movement to hide in. I think in the long run that was absolutely essential for my development.

SOPHIA: Their answers were inappropriate for you but the questions shifted your life. That's why I wouldn't dump on them the way I've heard other people do. If you take a historical perspective, you'll see that through history there have always been people who have stood on the extreme and everyone else scoffed, and said: 'They don't represent me'. But at least they have put forward the initial challenges to society.

AGNES: From a sociological perspective they may be valuable, but from a personal level they could be pretty destructive.

SOPHIA: I remember there were these heated debates about some of the older women because they cleaned the Centre. They actually used to wash the dishes and they used brooms and swept the place. Some people said that these women were hung up on housework, that they were valuing and glorifying it. But *they* said they refused to come into a house that stinks! *(Sophia laughs at the memory.)* You know, they weren't going to sit on a carpet that was flea-ridden.

BERNADETTE: And Bon Hull had signs up that said: 'Clean up your own shit'.

SOPHIA: That's right.

HELEN: I was standing in a queue for a film the other day, and I was behind two women that I recognised from the old days . . . they must have been in their sixties . . . and it was nice. We talked, and they are still very enthusiastic, but again, they've modified their positions.

SOPHIA: For me, it depends on who I'm talking to. I'm much more sensitive about alienating people, and I have no interest in calling myself a feminist in discussions where the other person is not going to listen.

SUE: The fact that I'm a feminist comes out in the conversation anyhow.

SOPHIA: Yes, of course, but it used to be *the* statement about my identity. Now it no longer is.

SUE: But I bet the man in your life would have to have the same sympathies and values about women as you do.

SOPHIA: Oh, yes. No one could ever be close to me without also accepting that I have views about women and women's role. They're views which I've acted on in a very public way over a period of years. But I have moved backwards. I've become much more cautious. I'm not as *fiercely* feminist now.

JANE: I don't necessarily call myself a feminist, but if someone asked me in a challenging way, I probably would say yes. But it comes through anyway. At work, particularly in male company, I just know it comes through. The biggest argument that goes on nowadays is the issue of using the word 'Ms'. I just can't believe how people get upset about it. I think it's very handy and I use it all the time. But some stupid people still ask if I'm ashamed to be married. And I can feel myself getting angry.

SOPHIA: 'Ms' is very significant because you have no dependent status. So you're saying: 'I'm separate from you. I don't need you to identify me'.

AGNES: Just thinking about labelling . . . you never hear anybody say 'authoress' or 'actress' anymore. They don't use diminutives.

SUE: No, it's like you can now be a person instead of a personess. *(Laughter.)*

BERNADETTE: I don't suppose I call myself a feminist. I know I believe in women's rights, but I don't always see issues in those terms. I've come to realise that I'm actually sexist too. That I'm sexist towards men and that I have sexist expectations of their role. I actually discovered that I see men as sexual objects too. *(General laughter.)* I've got this one friend and her husband is a feminist, or . . . whatever . . . and he picks me up on my sexism because I generalise against men like they used to generalise against women.

Actually I find that in a lot of ways men and women live in a different world, and men don't understand women. You know, mostly they work on a completely different wavelength altogether.

SOPHIA: I think there should have been a sex, a gender in-between men and women. We got either end, and I'm convinced they were supposed to give us something in the middle but they forgot.

BERNADETTE: But there are some people who accept both sides of themselves, the masculine and the feminine.

SUE: Well, feminism isn't a word that actually comes up except when it's a criticism unfortunately. If somebody asks if I'm a feminist . . . I'd say: 'I like to think so'.

I always regretted not getting more involved, although if it happened all over again I know I wouldn't be any different. I used to admire people who did the militant things. Even with my limited involvement I really do enjoy talking about those years. I love the look on people's faces when you tell them. Like it's really nice to have that bit of history. Something that was created in our time. I love it!

Interview 3: 15 June 1990
Rose

Once again Rose was unavailable to be interviewed with any of the other women. This session was conducted at her house. Rose began by talking about the differences between her marriage back in the '70s and her current relationship, which has lasted for over ten years. She believes that the communication is better now, but stresses that it's very difficult to compare two relationships which are so different.

Not only are the two men involved complete opposites, but her present partner has a serious illness which has changed him from the person he was when Rose first went out with him. The fact that he can no longer drink and go out at night has also meant a change from the kind of life they led earlier in their relationship. But on the question of expectations, Rose was philosophical.

ROSE: Well, I think you're always going to get some disappointments. Reality doesn't ever live up to what you thought it would be. At first everything is marvellous . . . you're in love . . . and then all of a sudden it settles down. You either accept it, or you don't. You can't change a person's personality. We still get on all right. It's not madly exciting or lustful, or anything like that.

Because he's ill, he has to rely on me for a lot. And we're just companions for each other. Like Darby and Joan really. I suppose I'm just content. Sex used to be very important to me. Now I wouldn't care if I never had it again. There is something else there that replaces it, a combination of things. Getting older has certainly had an effect on my libido. I don't know, maybe it's nature's way of settling us down. *(Rose has a gentle laugh at this idea.)*

I think my partner is much more domineering and aggressive than my husband was, but I usually stick up for myself. It doesn't upset me. And he tends to want to organise me. But it's not serious. There won't be any arguments, and he doesn't stop speaking to me. In fact he gives in very easily. So you've got this aggressiveness, but on the other hand he's quite gentle. He's like a big bear. *(Laughs.)* I don't feel disadvantaged or unequal at all.

With my children there was a bit of strain when I left my husband. My son was upset. He was twenty at the time, so he wasn't a kid. For my daughter it was a bit hard too. But they came good. They get on with my partner very well. The only problem was that I missed my son during that first year after I left, because he decided to stay at home with his father.

I would have really preferred another year on my own actually. But then things got tight for my partner financially, and he said: 'I can't keep it up unless you come and live here with me and we'll pay the house off together'. So that's what I did. It wasn't only a business arrangement, but if I'd had a choice, I would have stayed on my own much longer. I sort of got used to being on my own. But anyhow it seems to have worked out very well.

On the subject of friendships with women, Rose expressed sentiments that we had heard in the other interviews. She was generally more comfortable in the company of women than she had been before the group formed. She was more likely to confide in them and trust them. However, some of this new ease seemed to stem from her lack of interest in competing for attention from men.

ROSE: We're no beauties anymore. *(She chuckles.)* There are no men involved anymore. I'd had that experience of introducing my boyfriend to my girlfriends and they made eyes at him. That tended to make me a little cautious. It was pure jealousy, and insecurity. That doesn't seem to exist anymore. I don't think it will ever come back.

Asked if the CR group had affected her ability to relate to other women, Rose said that it had been one of several factors.

ROSE: Oh yes. Everything makes an impression on you to some extent. It's not just one thing. I can tell you I really missed the group when we stopped it. I really missed the women! I felt that we had friendship without getting too involved. Without sitting on each others' laps all the time. And yet we knew each other intimately. When I had that abortion, I was glad I had the group, because I would have been absolutely devastated without them.

In certain circumstances, you just need women friends. I'm probably more relaxed with women now than I've ever been, but I don't have that much time to spend with them these days.

Rose didn't have much to say on the subject of relationships with men, except that she doesn't 'see them as sex symbols anymore'. She has always found them easy to talk with and enjoyed their company, but now that her lifestyle has changed she has little opportunity to mix socially with them.

Back in the '70s, unlike most women at the time, Rose had been financially independent and accustomed to dealing with bankers and business people herself. She never had any problems with being assertive, although she did feel that she had been patronised by doctors at times. She also believes that she is sometimes treated differently by tradespeople who expect her to be ignorant because she's a woman.

ROSE: I can't argue with them if I don't know the facts well enough. I can't prove they've put one over on me. But you know when they're trying to put you down. I just don't go back to them.

Rose was unwilling to attribute changes in her life, her relationships, her attitudes and her self-esteem to her involvement with the CR group, or to any other single experience. She feels that age, more than anything, has relaxed and mellowed her, and changed her priorities. But she does believe that the women's movement was responsible for major social and political changes.

ROSE: The only thing I'm keen about now is the environment. I suppose you could call me a greenie in a way. I really get upset about animals, trees and those sorts of things. I really do! I think that's the next thing we have to concern ourselves with. It's one of our biggest issues.

For women, the change has been sort of a gradual thing. We don't have to be so militant now. I think we've achieved what we wanted on the social and political scene. Look how many women are in parliament now, and on T.V. and in journalism. Women are doing anything now . . . what used to be thought of as men's jobs.

They're in technical schools, they are doing trades now. And they weren't allowed to before.

I guess there are still businesses that discriminate against women. I'm not saying that it doesn't exist. But now everyone is aware of the Equal Opportunity Legislation, the Anti-Discrimination Act and the Sexual Harassment Act. There's some place to go with a complaint, and something to threaten them with. Before it was just . . . you know . . . you had to put up with it.

But I'm not really in the position to make comments on that. I've been in the one job year after year and I haven't had any hassles about anything. My job has always been done mostly by women. It's sort of a second job for a lot of people. A housewife's job. For a male to make it his career would be too boring. People don't take it seriously. Although you can get promoted, and I have been.

This led to a discussion about the nature of part-time work and the fact that it is mostly done by women, who are often attracted to jobs that allow them to look after children. The point was made that in many instances these jobs are not permanent, that they provide less superannuation and security, and they don't start women on real career paths or involve them in decision making.

ROSE: But then the way things are now, anybody can have jobs and conditions taken away from them. Unfortunately there's no security anymore for anybody, male or female. On the whole I think women are better off economically than they used to be. Of course it depends on the woman and what kind of job she's after, but the opportunities are there.

Probably the discrimination is there too, but it isn't as blatant as it used to be. There aren't as many things that irritate me now. The beauty contests seem to have nearly disappeared.

We discussed the possibility that because many issues of importance to women are less visible today, they no longer feel that they need to align themselves with feminism.

ROSE: Yes, there's a girl at work . . . a woman. Something came up one day and I said: 'That's what women's lib fought for,' and she said: 'Don't talk to me about that. I don't want to know about it. I don't like it'. That's one example that really hit me. I was only making a comment about wages and equal opportunities and I got that reaction from a woman.

I don't go around saying I'm a feminist. Not that they ask me. But obviously they know I am. Sometimes I just point things out . . . make comments, like: 'If I was a man you wouldn't speak to me like that'. Where I work I have to be careful. I would love to tell them off. But I can't offend the clients. One has to be diplomatic. We all have to survive.

Finally Rose was asked if she was satisfied with her life and herself.

ROSE: I think I could have done more with my life. Sort of educated myself more. Nothing prevented me really, except time and . . . I don't know . . . perhaps just lack of interest. Being short of money doesn't help either, you know. But there's no excuse. If you want to do something, you do it.

I never put something up there and said: 'That's my goal'. I never sort of formalised it. You know what I would have liked to be? A journalist. But I've always been scared of failure, and I end up not doing anything. Maybe I don't want to find out. *(Pause.)* I haven't really achieved that much, but perhaps I could say, I've achieved contentment with my own life.

Notes

Throughout this study, financial security emerged as the single most important determinant in how the women felt about themselves and what decisions they made.

An issue which surfaced in discussions about living with partners was the need for solitude. The women believed unanimously that occasional private time was essential within a healthy relationship.

They viewed being independent in a relationship as different from having enough solitude. Independence was seen as the reward for, first, financial and then emotional security. Privacy and space were thought of more as physical realities — a room, an afternoon, etc. — which had to be negotiated any time people shared their homes and lives. Most of the women had found their own ways of dealing with the trade-off between companionship and personal space.

Several of the women admitted they had rushed into new marriages or de facto partnerships for economic reasons rather than feelings of loneliness.

Bernadette was living alone by choice. Sophia was unattached, but confident about her new positive attitude to men. She was trying to imagine the ideal relationship for a woman who was both very independent and sometimes lonely. Rita was unable to say whether she was happier now than she had been in her marriage.

Most of the other women felt they were now in more satisfying relationships, either with new partners, or with the same partner in altered circumstances. Generally, they believed their levels of communication and intimacy with partners had improved, though several expressed regret about the difficulties men seem to have in simply talking things over.

All the women claimed to have more realistic expectations of relationships. The one exception was Rita who confessed to still believing Mr. Right might be out there somewhere.

Most of the women gave some credit for their improved relationships to the women's movement, which had taught them to take responsibility for themselves. This had raised their awareness of their personal power, making them able to actively choose more suitable partners, or in Helen's case, to work hard for a more satisfactory arrangement with her original partner.

In terms of personal power, as in expectations, Rita saw herself differently. The other women felt they exercised increased control over their lives, and were equals in decision-making which affected both partners. Conversely, Rita talked about being 'influenced' by those close to her, and about learning not to do anything 'dangerous'.

Where improved relationships did exist, the women agreed that their increased maturity was responsible in part. They were also quick to acknowledge the co-operation of their partners, especially the older and more conservative men, for whom adapting to the changing role of women had required a particular effort.

Ability to compromise appeared to be a major factor in the success of their relationships. Another was their greater self-awareness, which had enabled them to know which concessions couldn't be made without resentment. They joked about having acquired the ability to be selfish, demanding and independent, and as Jane said 'to be comfortable about that'.

Some women no longer regarded their relationship with a partner as the most important thing in their lives. Career goals and personal exploration had become central in some instances. Several spoke without regret of the less prominent position sex had in their lives now.

Equality, which was seen as a key feature of the best relationships, was inextricably linked to both parties being wage-earners. Where only one partner worked outside the home the women perceived an imbalance of power and control within that relationship.

There was a profound, if perverse, connection between status and earning capacity. For instance, Bernadette's former partner had felt threatened when she went into the paid workforce; it had created upheaval in their household's balance of power. Nevertheless, he had accorded her a higher status once she was at work than when she had been working at home.

The women uncovered this ambivalence in their own attitudes. Fifteen years ago they had been the ones who had resented their contribution in the home not being acknowledged as equal to that of their partners in the paid workforce. Some of those same women admitted feeling superior to their partners who were now retired. Not only did these women see themselves as more powerful than their unpaid spouses, but they considered themselves more valuable to society.

It was clear that these women viewed independence first and foremost in financial terms. Emotional independence was seen as something that resulted from financial equality and its impact on self-esteem.

It was equally clear that some of them were their own worst enemies when it came to relinquishing aspects of their traditional roles. This meant they carried an unequal share of the domestic chores on the 'second shift', regardless of what they did in the paid workforce.

Everyone agreed that the most unsettling factor in relationships with new partners was the existence of the woman's children. As Sue lamented, 'Having kids that aren't your partner's causes more tension than anything'. Gloria added 'and the person who bears the brunt of things is usually the mother'.

Some of the women questioned whether the nature of a man's feeling for his children could ever be as strong as a mother's, but both Rita and Bernadette believed their ex-husbands were as bonded to their children as they were themselves. Helen said that she deliberately sought to play a more dominant role in her son's upbringing and education than his father.

We found that most of the women now see themselves differently in relation to professionals who have traditionally been icons of authority, such as doctors, lawyers and bankers. Maturity and financial independence were once again cited as the reasons the women felt more capable of asserting themselves in these relationships.

Knowledge was another contributing factor. On the whole the women see themselves as better informed about traditionally male power structures in general, and in particular about law, finance and health. For this much of the credit was given to the women's movement, although several of the women pointed out that women who worked in these fields were as capable of paternalism as men.

Getting old was an important issue for everyone. On the whole the women were positive about ageing and recognised it's advantages. They talked about the freedom that came with decreased family responsibilities. They seemed at least philosophical, at best happy, about having undergone a process of mellowing, of getting things into perspective. Some spoke of having replaced feelings of hostility and alienating behaviour with a quieter, deeper confidence. They looked forward to the challenges ahead of them.

But as with almost every other issue, there were competing forces which influenced their attitudes to ageing. There was a general belief that with age they had outgrown their vulnerability to other people's opinions of them. On the other hand they were realistic about living in, and being conditioned by, a culture which glorifies youth.

The women in this study reflected both the pride of the survivor and the anxiety of the redundant. Occasionally, discrepancies between their statements underlined that tension. Gloria commented that she had 'never felt better' and that she 'felt younger than [she] did twenty years ago', but later talked about curtailing her activities these days because of tiredness.

For some more than others, there were the inevitable fears about loss of physical attractiveness. Some women paid vigorous lip service to their right to relax about themselves after decades of trying to live up to other people's ideals. Some even wanted to embrace their expanding waistlines and greying hair along with their slowing pace. But they were outnumbered.

In practice, no one was completely immune to the message in the maxim that women can never be good enough, so they must never stop trying to be good enough. Not one person seriously suggested that the hours and dollars they devoted to looking good (young) could have been spent on solving more important problems.

Paradoxically, some of the women who were most vocal about celebrating their maturity occasionally doubted their own motives. They allowed for the possibility that they might be kidding themselves, simply making the best of a situation they were powerless to change.

There were no such reservations about the nexus between image, age and employment. The whole group was adamant that they had more to offer an employer now, in terms of understanding, poise, experience, and reliability, than when they were younger. On the other hand, they knew employers remain unconvinced, and they felt it would be foolish to ignore this reality. While they deplored the prejudices which made it necessary, most were willing to lie about their birthdate if it gave them a better shot at a job.

In conversation the women mentioned movie stars who had managed to combine ageing with box office acceptability. No one believed these celebrities represented the average ageing woman any more than in their youth they had represented the average young woman. While for some they were role models, others pointed out that they were acceptable precisely because they didn't look like 'older women'. They were not so much valued for their character and maturity, as in spite of it.

Where does the women's movement come into this? Nobody claimed it had prepared them to feel good about growing old, but what did emerge was the link between their general sense of being 'okay' now, and the contribution that consciousness-raising had made to their confidence and self-esteem years ago. Helen referred to this when she commented that 'there comes a time when you look in the mirror and you see your wrinkles, and it's very important, when you get to that stage, to have sorted out how you feel about yourself'.

When we asked the women if they called themselves feminists today most felt it necessary to make a number of qualifications, including personal definitions of feminism, before answering.

Most said the matter rarely if ever came up overtly, though some were sure other people considered them to be feminists. This was not necessarily a compliment, and seemed based on perceptions of them as aggressive. Sue and Jane felt their feminism was obvious in their behaviour and conversations, but neither seemed to have much to do with women, apart from each other.

Some gave examples of how they put feminist principles into practice. These ranged from outings with other women to non-sexist domestic structures and climbs up the corporate ladder. Some of the women kept themselves well-informed about changes in legislation and public opinion which had an impact on women. Some attended the occasional women's seminar or conference.

No one took part in anything which could be called feminist activism. Reasons for this ranged from shifting priorities to activist burnout and the appropriateness of handing over the reins to the next generation of women. Only Agnes felt that she was a more committed feminist today because she was less introspective than she had been when the group met.

There was a powerful link between the women's self-image and their willingness to call themselves feminists. Predictably, some were shy of the lesbian tag which has always been attached to avowed feminists. They explained that it was not lesbians, but inaccurate labelling which they rejected.

This has been an issue for heterosexual women from the beginning. In part it is a result of the community's genuine ignorance, which in turn is due to a manipulative use of red herrings by unimaginative opponents of the women's movement. Jane remembered her husband saying 'Kids, your mother's off with her lezzie friends' as she prepared to leave for a CR meeting. Most of the women could contribute a similar anecdote.

Some women believed that due to portrayal by the media, the general public equated feminism with aggression and hatred of men. They were afraid feminists were seen as having no respect for other people's deepest feelings and most cherished traditions.

These misconceptions and generalities were enough to discourage them from associating themselves with feminism.

This stigmatisation was demonstrated in a 1991 vox populi segment on a commercial television station. Young Australian women stated that, based on what they understood feminism to mean, they wanted nothing to do with it. It was a bitter reminder of one of the reasons we had decided to write this book in the first place.

Attitudes of, and about, younger women are discussed at some length in the next chapter.

What things look like from here

> In which the women discuss: the reunion as a mirror; the 'blancmange of before'; the '70s context; did we win the war?; the case of the disappearing movement; mid-life crisis; legislation and reality; today's issues; why did we stop?; memory; sisterhood; being in a book, and much more.

Getting people who knew each other twenty years ago to come together again meant asking them to confront aspects of their lives in quite a public way. By agreeing to take part in the project the women allowed us not just to observe the course their lives had taken, but to intrude on, and to some degree change, their present lives.

We were interested primarily in their appraisal of the women's movement: its successes and failures, its future if any. But we also wanted to know how they felt about having the spotlight shining on them for the purpose of this study.

The women in the group had some questions for us too, so in this chapter we departed from the conversational style of the previous sessions in favour of one-to-one interviews. We appear in this chapter both as group members using assumed names and as interviewers. (We interviewed each other.) This device was adopted so that we could participate both as subjective group members, and when appropriate, as more objective editors and project co-ordinators. In practice, it proved to be a very useful way of helping us make that mental and emotional shift from subject to object and back again.

Bernadette
11 June 1990

BERNADETTE: It's been really good to see everyone again; to see the changes and the growth that nearly everybody has gone through. They've come from being housewives and being very identified with that role, to opening right out and becoming part of the world. So it's been great, catching up with people who were in the group.

When you first contacted me about the project I was going through a very angry period. I wasn't thinking about anybody else so much as my own anger . . . and . . . I guess I don't feel like I've put a lot into the project. It brought up a lot of disappointments. You know, it put me in the position of looking back over the past twenty years and evaluating what's happened to me from that point to this point and how the women's movement affected that. And, well . . . it didn't seem very positive. Of course now I can look at it a bit differently.

But what I really wanted was a traditional sort of lifestyle, and I've never achieved that. I haven't even been able to have a good relationship. I do have a home which I can offer my children. I've done that all by myself. It's not from anybody else. And that's a huge achievement. It's really good just being able to manage . . . I feel quite happy with that now. But I feel like I've never really found my own direction as a person.

INTERVIEWER: Have you still got that hankering after the traditional role?

BERNADETTE: Well, I think I'm getting to the stage where I'm not sure those were such good goals anyhow. But I don't really know what I want. I mean, I still find it hard to put myself and what I want to achieve before the other things in my life. Being involved with the project brought my frustration to the surface. I suppose it's the mid-life crisis too. I have become independent, but I haven't taken the extra steps toward being independent in a creative way, you know. I see what other people have done and I think, *Wow! It's so fantastic.* Through being involved with the women's movement they've really become aware of what they wanted out of life and they've gone for it and they've got it.

INTERVIEWER: We noticed a big difference in you last time we saw you. I think we'd forgotten that changes are going on all the time. We hadn't given much thought to what it meant to come into someone's life at one point and record how they felt, and to do it again two years later. Yes, you seem to be in a very different space now.

BERNADETTE: Thank heavens!

INTERVIEWER: If you look back at the whole women's movement, not just our CR group, do you think it had any lasting value?

BERNADETTE: Yes, I think it made a great difference in a very wide sense. I remember when I was a teenager there was no information about sex or contraceptives or abortion . . . or just about the fact that people have the right to make those sorts of decisions for themselves. And there were no rape crisis centres. So socially it has made a lot of difference to people who don't even know now where these things come from. They're all taken for granted now but their origin was the women's movement.

I know there are lots of things that haven't changed but there's usually an option available if someone doesn't fit the stereotype now, and there are more teachers and people presenting alternatives and pushing kids into opening up ways of looking at themselves which didn't exist before the women's movement. So I think it's had a great impact, and a positive one too.

But I think it's been used. I think a lot of women are under pressure to be independent now, and they're going to have the health consequences that result from higher stress levels, because of all the demands on them. But . . . I mean . . . that's the way the world's going and there's not much that I can do about it. But I don't like it. *(She laughs.)*

INTERVIEWER: I'm just curious about something. You said that when you joined the consciousness-raising group you were surprised that the content of the meetings was more personal than political. And then you said later that there were lots of personal issues for you that you didn't examine during that period. What's the connection between those statements?

BERNADETTE: Well, I went into it thinking that we had to change things in a wider sense, outside ourselves rather than inside. But we didn't. We got together and we talked about our personal lives . . . I didn't really see how they were related at the time.

And I don't know if I was really able to look at myself honestly then. I don't know that I'm much better now but I've been forced to realise things about myself in the meantime. Does that make sense?

INTERVIEWER: Of course. When I look back over these recordings, I realise that each woman had her own personal reasons for being in that group, depending on what she most needed.

BERNADETTE: And sometimes it's much easier to go out and do some work and help somebody . . . to rally to a cause for an ideal . . . than to really examine yourself and your own life honestly. That's a lot more difficult and it takes a different sort of energy. You can't just fix the things in your own life. There's a long process of exploration and . . . muddle?

Here Bernadette interviews the interviewer.

Have you had to ask yourselves these questions?

INTERVIEWER: Yes, we asked each other the questions. We haven't been passive observers. We tried to arrange things so that we wouldn't always have to be objective.

Groping for our own answers helped us understand what it was we were trying to find out from the rest of you, and it helped us formulate better questions. You'd expect us to already know our own answers, but it didn't really work that way. We both discovered things about ourselves. It was like a personal stocktaking. I found the early interviews fairly unsettling, because it had been a long time since I'd talked with people on that level. And that helped me to understand the misgivings somebody like Sophia had. But in the long run it's been exhilarating.

BERNADETTE: Have you got a lot out of it? It sounds like you have.

INTERVIEWER: A tremendous amount. Like you, I was curious about what had become of everyone. I confess that over the years I hadn't spent a lot of time thinking about these women, which is odd when you know how close we once were.

On that first day, the reunion, I was in my lounge room looking at all these women sitting around, and I thought, *Nothing's changed!* Of course there had been changes, but not to the sense of feeling okay about being together . . . We all looked at each other with that same kind of curiosity I think. There was a lot of sizing up and sussing out. But before very long we were laughing and carrying on just as though no time had passed.

So now . . . I'm very proud of all of us. I still feel very connected to all of you. Our experience together is something unrepeatable. We'll never do that again. And not one person said she couldn't come back for the project. You know, I'm pretty bowled over by that.

BERNADETTE: And there's also the confidentiality. That's always been respected. Any one of us could have . . .

INTERVIEWER: . . . blown the whistle. *(They both laugh.)*

BERNADETTE: Exactly! And yet it never even crossed anybody's mind. It was really important that we could just agree to something like that and stick to it. Which says something pretty amazing, given that we had fights . . . disagreements. And we still have.

INTERVIEWER: Yes, that hasn't changed.

BERNADETTE: I think that by saying you're allied with the women's movement you're taking responsibility and making your own rules. You're saying: 'My experience is valid and I'm valid, and I don't have to give my power to the Church, or to men or to some political group; I'm taking that power myself'. By being a feminist, that's what you're doing, you're recognising your power as a person — as a woman person.

At times within the movement there was an attempt to define what a real feminist was, but within our group that wasn't at all the way. We supported each other, really, didn't we? Against that.

Also, as feminists we've banned together to do something about oppression in the outside world, and the prejudices particularly levelled against women. Like Zelda D'Aprano chaining herself to the Commonwealth Building gates to protest for equal pay. People have done those sorts of brave public things. That was a part of it too, as well as the personal thing.

Actually it looks like a lot of things are going backwards in America. It can happen here too. Then people will have to fight for those rights all over again. They've been won for now, but they could be taken away again.

Sophia
8 July 1990

SOPHIA: The first thing that comes to mind is something I learned in the early '70s at university. It was the old Marxist theory about history being very important. It informs your activity and it informs the future. And after these months of discussion with the group I can see how important the decisions of the past have been in terms of the decisions I'm making now in my life.

Secondly, it's been a major re-affirmation of my identity and the elements which have formed my identity. It's inevitable that you change; you exhaust certain spheres of activity in your life and you move into new ones, and you tend to forget how those earlier activities have shaped you.

You have allowed me to look back and gain a sense of what was happening to me as an individual first . . . just as a human being . . . through the '70s, and through the whole women's liberation movement. It's given me a very strong context for what I'm doing now and it's great! I just feel so . . . I suppose . . . complete.

That may seem a strange thing to say for someone who's thirty-eight and single. And it doesn't negate what I said in previous interviews about regretting certain choices that I made in the '70s. But the project has allowed me to reflect on whether it was all worthwhile? And my conclusion is that I've actually been part of a very, very important period in history, and that experience was a very rewarding growth and development milestone in my life. So *(looking around the room)* thank you very much.

INTERVIEWER: This is a good time for me to get you to correct an impression if it was a false one. On the day of the reunion you showed up in high heels, tight skirt, long red fingernails . . . I figured there was a message in that for us. And when we started talking I sensed you wanted us to understand that the period of your life when you'd been very committed to the women's movement was over, and that you viewed even talking about it again as painful, tiresome and totally irrelevant today. Was that a more or less accurate impression?

SOPHIA: Yes. Yes. I've always had a fear of being boxed in to an identity that people will not allow me to change. There's a natural tendency for people to say: 'That's how we knew Sophia then and she has to be consistent.' I guess I was really intimidated because I felt I'd changed. So, yes, you're right. I really had a very strong fear of you wanting to drag me back to my past. I must have been as prickly as a porcupine.

INTERVIEWER: Later you went through a profound period of reappraisal and change. This seems to have followed quickly after the reunion. Is that a coincidence, or was it connected at all to us asking a whole lot of questions about the past?

SOPHIA: Well, I want to give the group, and the process, the major credit for the transformation. What you did, my dear, was strike me at the point of the big reassessment. You know, the sort of mid-life crisis or whatever you like to call it.

INTERVIEWER: If we were going to get you that was a good time?

SOPHIA: Yeah. When that initial contact was made things were still firing for me in terms of objectives I'd set myself through the 'eighties. You know, becoming much more successful. My personal income was still expanding, and my power base still growing.

But not too long after that I realised I'd had a very strong yen for probably three or four years to make a break with the organisational world. I had my home, and I didn't really want much more, other than things that were going to be stimulating . . . things I found that money and success couldn't buy.

And it was interesting, because, remember, I came to you when I went through the job crisis. I once again felt that bonding, that link and understanding. I could very quickly pick it up again after all those years, and . . . therefore, in an interesting sort of way, this project facilitated that crisis. I mean if the group . . . if the discussions hadn't come up again, I still would have been going through the crisis. I can say that's been the key contribution.

Note: *Sophia married in 1991 and had a baby in 1992.*

Jane
4 July 1990

JANE: I think that it was a tremendous movement for freeing women up and fighting for women's rights. I don't even know if it exists these days. It was terrific at the time and it meant something to me, but I have no thoughts and feelings about it now. I don't have any bad memories about it either.

INTERVIEWER: So you think it's all over?

JANE: It is certainly not as necessary as it used to be. I think that the changes in society need to continue. There are still huge areas of discrimination against females and some people have very sexist attitudes. But society has changed dramatically and it will continue to change. I don't know if it still needs the women's movement anymore.

INTERVIEWER: You mentioned changes that need to continue. What are they?

JANE: Maybe with the less educated women and possibly with migrant women. I don't know, I have no exposure to them. But in the average Australian girl's life, I think that all the changes have occurred. They are much more aware of options and they are less inclined to be rigidly fixed in their old roles.

INTERVIEWER: How different are you from the woman you were twenty years ago?

JANE: Certainly there has been a change from that questioning . . . very radical attitude (at least for me it was radical) back into a more complacent acceptance. I certainly don't tackle people on those issues anymore like I used to. And in some cases I turn a blind eye I guess to some things that are discriminatory, and I mightn't have done that before. But that's an ageing thing anyhow. The angry young person and then the complacent middle-aged one. It occurs no matter what.

INTERVIEWER: Were you at all reluctant about being in this project?

JANE: No, no. The only thing it did was raise the question of whether perhaps I'd sold myself out in the end on all those issues? But I don't know that there was enough in that to make me feel really disappointed.

Perhaps I asked myself whether, considering all that effort and time, I'd created enough change in myself to fit the ideal I'd had . . . maybe we all had . . . back in the '70s. Would I be seen . . . or would I see myself . . . as having gone through that huge christening and then having settled back to the 'blancmange' of before?

I guess I might have been concerned about that when we first met again. There was a certain element of that. If we'd had very radical people in the group, I think I would have felt that I might be judged harshly by them if they were still carrying the banner.

INTERVIEWER: Well, look at Germaine Greer. When I read some of her recent articles, I feel quite disappointed. She abandoned us. *(Laughs.)* She mellowed too.

JANE: Also perhaps she came to the conclusion that you can only go on banging the same drum for so long without becoming tedious. And I know when I meet women, not young women necessarily, older women who discovered the idea of feminism and equality later in life, they can be quite tedious. They have very strident behaviour. I don't know if we came across like that to people, but if we did it's no wonder we upset them.

INTERVIEWER: Do you think the women's movement and the group were actually worthwhile? Did anything change because of them?

JANE: Were they worthwhile for me personally? Absolutely! I think the women's movement came just at the time when I was about to break out. Maybe I would have never done it otherwise. Maybe I wouldn't have had the courage without the group. For me it was just perfect. I changed my life so dramatically from being a housewife in an unhappy marriage, with no prospects and three kids under four years old, to a mature woman who is the only female executive in my organisation. You could say I'm a success story.

For women in general, it's harder to see the total connection between the movement and the way the world has changed. Lots of things are responsible. The women's movement had an effect on government legislation, and that legislation is intertwined with all those changes in education that meant you got women and men in schools who had more liberal views and attitudes on equality. In turn they imparted those views to the kids, and so the world is changing. And people that are in a position to make legislative changes are products of the educational system that the women's movement, or the feeling of the time, had an effect on.

So the movement was there. It was creating an effect. But not in a clear cut way. Perhaps it was just part of a total ground swell of change, like the moratorium for the Vietnam War. Who can say. I think society was just changing.

Tell me, why did we actually stop the meetings; was it a joint decision? What was the reason for it? Because I really could have gone on. I can't remember how we actually ended. But I felt it was a pity because I enjoyed the group so much. Also, it's a bit sad that we never met again. All these years and we were so close.

Sue
12 July 1990

INTERVIEWER: What has it been like for you to look at yourself as you were twenty years ago and as you are now?

SUE: I'm disappointed in myself. It made me feel sad that even in myself I'd let things die. All the things that I thought were so important, I'd let slip. I was saddened a bit by my own lack of involvement. I don't know if it was the disappearance of the group . . . we needed that sort of thing . . . we were being fed by it all the time. I loved the involvement when the group was there. I loved the fact that one had to think. And the thing I loved most about the women was that they were non-judgmental.

INTERVIEWER: Yes, that comes through very strongly from everybody. And . . . it's strange . . . another thing came through from the others. Nobody can remember why we stopped?

SUE: Yes, again, I think it was just at that stage of our lives when the pursuits were very large. Some were studying, and some were involved in new partnerships . . . you couldn't do everything. And you felt that it was . . . not finished . . . but that it had helped and it was something we didn't need as much.

INTERVIEWER: Yes, I agree. I've been trying hard to remember my feelings at the time. I think I had other things to do and I'd got from the group what I needed.

SUE: It was almost like the end of a project. Like your project here.

INTERVIEWER: Yes, something that moved us towards a goal rather than just raising our consciousness. But was it worthwhile? Not just the group, but the whole movement?

SUE: Yes, it was worthwhile. Although at times it messed my life up. When the marriage ended my husband was so vitriolic about the effect the group had had on my life. According to him, you know, it had changed me. And it probably did, but the marriage wasn't right. It had nothing to do with the movement. Absolutely nothing at all.

Because you become more outspoken about what you expect out of life it comes out of your mouth . . . over and over and over again. I make much more noise about things that I feel are going wrong in a relationship. I've become independent. And it causes problems still. It will never stop causing problems in our age group.

But the movement just broadened so many people's lives. Men's too, even though they fought it. It made them aware of a lot of things they hadn't been aware of before.

INTERVIEWER: How do you feel about the women's movement now?

SUE: Unfortunately it seems to have disappeared. I think it's up to us to remind people of it . . . the young kids especially. They've forgotten that so much work has been done. So I think that's important. And I feel there will be a resurgence of the interest that's lapsed over the last few years. I hope so.

I think there always have to be extreme people, because most of us just wait for something to be done. I mean, some women used to have to chain themselves to buildings so we could get the vote. So unfortunately feminists are thought of as being weird. It's always the bra-burning remark; it never ceases to amaze me that people remember that one thing and we're all thought of as rather weird.

I was telling a young girl in the office the other day that I had been weird for years, and I was angry all the time. But it was because of the anger that the message got through to my family and my friends. I haven't got a daughter; I just wish I did, so I could see how my thoughts and feelings would have affected her. But I think they affected my sons. I'm hoping there will be another rush of activism that my children can be involved in.

INTERVIEWER: You can always start one, you know.

SUE: No, I told you, I was never one to start anything.

Agnes
16 December 1990

INTERVIEWER: How do you feel these days about the women's movement? Did it accomplish anything?

AGNES: Yes, certainly, in some ways the world is a much more welcoming place for my daughter than it was for me when I was her age. It tolerates difference better, thanks largely to the women's movement. I know there were other things going on back in the '70s, but I was so bogged down in my own concerns then that I didn't really think about Vietnam or politics until after I got involved with a movement that promised me some hope of changing personal things. The women's movement politicised millions of ordinary housewives.

People have talked about how exciting those days were, but I also think they were frightening in some ways. History was on a cusp in the '70s. Old values were being chucked out and huge changes were taking place very fast. This was especially true where the role of women was concerned, because the feminist debate encompassed most of those questions that were being asked on the other activist fronts. Questions about sexuality, population, the human propensity for violence, the rights of the individual and the need to take public stands — women were looking at all these things. Questions about who held the power, not just globally but in the house, the doctor's office, the school, the media . . .

I sometimes felt like I was on a roller-coaster ride, hurtling along at great speed, climbing and then dropping suddenly, and not actually able to control where I went or when I stopped. And I was a little afraid of where I was going. I often thought of myself as the most tentative woman in the group. But in the long term, I did take control of my own . . . trip.

INTERVIEWER: So do you see a role for the women's movement today, or do you think it has outlived its usefulness?

AGNES: If you mean marching in overalls and power-fist salutes, I'd have to say I think those things are anachronisms. I'd like to believe feminism isn't tied to the past by virtue of the music and the clothes, or the dialectic reserved for discussing the issues. I'd like to think that a feminist way of looking at the world would transcend fashion and move with the times.

What I think must definitely be preserved is a feminist consciousness that keeps women on their toes and watchful for threats to what we've gained. As well as the knowledge that keeps women aware of the strength they can gain from each other.

And I'm sure that there are just as many issues for us to be concerned with today as there were twenty years ago. There are still great discrepancies between the way men and women are treated by welfare agencies, Social Security, the courts. And the media, my god! They show us a few women in shoulder pads cooking dinner for one, and that's supposed to make up for all the White Wings Mums and the tits and bums and the model newsreaders and the dizzy blonde game show hostesses and the weight-loss rip-offs on daytime programs. If anybody thinks we've won the fight for once and for all, let them watch a couple of hours of television. And let them be aware that our children are watching a great deal more than that.

We have to be concerned about domestic violence, and violence outside the home, and violent pornography. We have to be aware that the victims are almost always women and to ask why. These aren't old issues, they're depressingly current and getting worse.

There are still economic areas to look at, real equity in the workforce, superannuation, the 'glass ceiling'. There's the question of equal representation in business and politics. It worries me that individual women who have achieved success in these terms tend to deny the problem exists. We have to guard against the divisions that kind of thinking creates. We have to try and stay united without being uniform.

INTERVIEWER: What has it been like for you participating in these interviews and seeing all your old friends again after so long?

AGNES: It's been great to see everyone again, and to find out how they've developed over the years. It's been more like a family reunion than a reunion of friends. There have been some surprises. But if I'd ever had any doubts about just how significant the CR group was, I wouldn't have them now.

I really feel sisterhood was so powerful that even the reluctant ones were willing to help you with this book. And when we did come together, there was an acknowledgement that we had that unique relationship. Even the ones who seem to have given up the women's movement still feel connected to the women from the group.

I love having that bond that's stronger than our individual differences. But I won't minimise those differences either. Some of my old mates have . . . mellowed . . . They don't seem to care about things the way they once did. That surprised me because I actually care more, but then I was pretty self-concerned in the '70s. Maybe my timing is just out of sync with other middle-aged ladies.

It's been a chance to see my own experience in some kind of context. More than one context actually. There was the social-historical one, and the personal one of a confused, inhibited twenty-four-year-old. Aspects of my behaviour make a lot more sense to me in retrospect.

Rose
15 June 1990

ROSE: In the long term, I think the women's movement achieved what it set out to do. It achieved a lot socially and politically.

INTERVIEWER: Do you think there is anything more to be done?

ROSE: I don't feel that strongly about anything. Perhaps child abuse. A lot more's got to be done about that, but I don't know if it's tied up with the women's movement. Though most of the offenders are male. And of course wife bashing. We could do a lot more about that. And rape — the rape crisis centres need to go on.

INTERVIEWER: You've got them at every university and hospital now.

ROSE: Yes, that's something that came out of the movement. And the child abuse and the wife-bashing issues seem to be talked about a lot, where before they were all sort of hushed up. I don't know. I'm out of touch with what goes on. You see, I used to be in the union. You know what's going on then, but I'm not in it anymore.

INTERVIEWER: Your life has changed a lot since the group split up. What has it been like for you to see everybody again after all this time?

ROSE: I think it was good. I'd forgotten some things. I liked meeting the other women and finding out what had happened to them.* It had been nearly fifteen years. That means all the things we've been through . . . all the dramas and the traumas, and each time you have one you cope. So it was a positive experience.

But then there were a couple who didn't feel that way, weren't there? That surprised me at first, but I think I can understand it now. If you've changed a lot you might be embarrassed to talk about how you used to be.

INTERVIEWER: Well, we probably all felt there were things we would rather not talk about. There were things I did in 1972 that seem silly today.

ROSE: So how did *you* actually feel about doing the project?

INTERVIEWER: From the first time we talked about the project over a cup of coffee I was sure I wanted to do it. And then at the reunion I felt as if there weren't fifteen years that had passed. I could talk to all of you as if the group had never stopped. It's like a good friendship, you don't need to see each other every day. Certainly I'd have

---

* Note: Rose has always been interviewed by herself. Here she is referring to the reunion and social dinners we had.

to say for me it was one of the most enjoyable and satisfying experiences to interview and talk to all of you.

ROSE: Did the women's movement and the group have anything to do with the career you're in now? You know, you went on and did things. Was that because of the movement or because of other things?

INTERVIEWER: Part of it was the movement. Let's say that I always knew I'd go back to the workforce when my child was a certain age. I was always a bit ambitious. I already had professional qualifications, but I wanted to improve my job opportunities. That's why I went back to study. I think the movement and the group gave me the push. So many women returned to study. Nearly everybody in the group did something. So, partly it was the women's movement, partly my own development . . . and, you know . . . partly the '70s.

Gloria
26 June 1990

GLORIA: I don't think the women's movement is all over. It may be going along quietly but it's not over. I think we still have such a long way to go.

It's sort of a non-issue in a lot of places . . . people just don't seem to be aware. Ten years ago there was much more in the newspaper, in the media. I think at the moment the economic climate is so bad that it seems to take over everything. The whole country is going down. Of course women are going to suffer more than anybody.

I feel the younger generation of women have a different set of values. Many are not interested in being equal individuals. They are more interested in material gains, social status perhaps through their husbands. There are so many things opening up to them that were traditionally male . . . engineering, the arts, the media.

But when they get married, they still come home and do the housework. Or at least most of it.

I don't think they are searching inside themselves, questioning lifestyle, role models and so on. They're really scared to make waves. They are happy at the moment to enjoy the status quo. They are becoming too complacent and perhaps too lazy.

I think unless they're careful, there will be a slide back from feminism. They aren't aware of what it was like twenty, thirty years ago when women weren't allowed to own property. And when you wanted a loan, even if you earned good money, you needed a male to go guarantor for you. That was only about ten years ago. Some people growing up these days think that can't happen again. But you never know.

It depends on the individual, but I think a lot of women are still quite happy to be sort of a second-class citizen, attached to some male. Perhaps I'm too hard on them. Perhaps I'm judging it from my standard.

INTERVIEWER: What issues do you think the movement should be concentrating on today?

GLORIA: I think there is still a problem with attitudes catching up with legislation. And there is a lot of ignorance about how to use the new laws regarding equal opportunity, sexual harassment, etc. The system doesn't make it easy for people. They often don't know how to go about getting justice for themselves. That should be taught in the schools. Not just to the girls. There should be a whole subject that teaches the people in this country their rights.

INTERVIEWER: What were your impressions that first time we got together again?

GLORIA: It was fascinating. It was as though no time had gone by. So obviously our hopes, desires and personalities were all such that we could still be friends. We had the interest in common, although our lives had gone in different directions. I think we would have always been drawn together. We were back in the '70s because of circumstances. The circumstances are different now, but we're still the same people.

INTERVIEWER: Were you at all anxious about coming together again?

GLORIA: No, I wasn't. Perhaps from your side it was different because you were trying to write a book. But I was just . . . I guess . . . curious and excited to see everybody. Wondering what we all had achieved. How we'd changed physically. I thought it was very exciting, like a challenge. No, I wasn't nervous at all. *(Laughs.)* But . . . well, I guess this is vanity . . . I wanted to look my age, not mutton dressed up as lamb. In the end I made no special effort but I thought about it a lot.

INTERVIEWER: Yes, we did the same thing, and we giggled at ourselves for it. Did you learn anything by comparing yourself today with what you were like twenty years ago?

GLORIA: Well, it wasn't disturbing or uncomfortable because I'm doing it all the time. I think about my life in the past and where I was going and where I'm at now. And also where I'm going in the future. Perhaps by us meeting again and discussing all these things, it made me more conscious of taking stock.

Look, I must also add what it did do for me. It sort of inspired me to keep trying. Keep fighting for my individuality. Sometimes I feel like I'm weakening.

INTERVIEWER: Well, you said at the reunion that you were very happy, but a bit worried that you'd become complacent. You're so content you don't risk stirring things up.

GLORIA: Yes, that was at a stage in my life when I was aware of becoming too smug. Sort of settling into life and saying everything is marvellous. And sometimes when you feel like that you aren't striving, you stagnate. I don't feel like that now because I've realised there is still so much that I want to do with my life. That's partly because of being in the interviews and talking a lot to people who are receptive. Yes, I think I was a bit scared of stagnating. I'm not anymore. That was two years ago. I feel I'm even more alert now.

INTERVIEWER: That's the interesting thing with this project. There have been tremendous changes in some of you since we started it. Even within two years women can develop, change again.

GLORIA: Perhaps for some it brought up too much. Something happened with Rita that made her want to retreat. But I certainly didn't have any negative feelings. No, it was wonderful! It's exciting!

INTERVIEWER: What about the group and the movement in retrospect? Did they accomplish anything?

GLORIA: Oh for me, for sure, because until I belonged to the women's movement I was an isolated individual rebelling against society. I'd been told by my family that I was selfish, abnormal, mad. When I realised that there were so many women who felt exactly the same . . . who put into words what my feelings were . . . I knew I wasn't unreasonable for wanting to improve my life.

I've often thought about this: would I have had the confidence to go to college if I hadn't felt what I was doing was right and normal? There were so many women looking for answers about their lives, and I was just one more. So the movement was good for women in general.

That was also a time when suddenly a lot of things were possible. The universities and colleges opened up for mature-age women because the fees were abolished. There was the NEAT scheme [National Education and Training Scheme]. Whatever you think about the Whitlam years, he made all those things possible, and it changed my life. I couldn't have gone otherwise.

INTERVIEWER: You're not an isolated case. I remember at uni, we had so many mature-age women studying . . . and leaving their husbands right, left and centre.

GLORIA: *(Laughs.)* I think I told you, when I went to college there were sixty married ladies. When I left at the end of three years thirty of us had got divorced. I know what happened to me. I got financial security.

INTERVIEWER: Yes, it really comes back to economic independence and that gives you power. Let's face it, if you don't have your own money, there is really nothing you can undertake.

GLORIA: Yes, I was financially independent and also I was older and more able to cope emotionally. I thought teaching would be the most marvellous career anybody could have, and for me it was and still is a vocation. Not only was I going to earn money but I would also be fulfilled in the area of my work.

I think it's wonderful that you're writing this book. I hadn't made any attempts to contact people. We were so close at one stage, and yet I was willing to let these lives go off and not know anything about what happened to them. I think it's marvellous that we all have got together and seen where we've gone.

INTERVIEWER: Well, we felt it was so important to have that documented somehow. We don't want to postulate any theories or anything. Just to record what happened to a group of ordinary women. We weren't really militant feminists, but ordinary middle-class women, living in middle-class suburbs with middle-class values.

GLORIA: But obviously dissatisfied with our lives and looking for some answers.

INTERVIEWER: . . . and they needed to be women's answers, not male answers. We went through so much, and people were so negative about what we were doing. But we survived.

Helen
29 September 1990

INTERVIEWER: Can you give me a retrospective on the women's movement?

HELEN: I feel it was a necessary historical development . . . like civil rights, especially those of minority groups . . . the anti-war movement. It developed in a time of questioning those in power, especially world powers. Of course it was still a time of full employment. People didn't have to worry about jobs so much. They could direct their energy towards looking at society . . . at what improvements could be made.

In the '70s the women's movement was out in the open. Women were proud of their initiatives and actions, full of enthusiasm like children bursting out with ideas and energy, spreading the message like evangelists or missionaries. We were convinced that there would be a new world order. We never doubted that. At least I never doubted it.

I trusted the movement completely. Now the movement seems to have disappeared, though I think it just works in a different way. We don't have that concerted or collective effort anymore. We don't work so much from the group base anymore, but I do think that women as individuals quietly carry on the fight. We stand up where we feel we have to. When discrimination affects us personally, or when we feel that some injustice has been committed against a woman, we act, but on a more personal level. Like talking to the woman, or writing a letter to the editor of a newspaper. I know that's how I carry on the fight.

So, I think the fight for equal rights is still going on . . . out there individually by some known or unknown sisters. I still feel part of it and I still feel proud of it and proud of having taken part in an historical fight.

INTERVIEWER: Some people think we've seen the end of the

movement, but you sound as though you think there are still things worth fighting for.

HELEN: I don't think we've seen the end. Sure we have legislation in regard to equal pay, and so that we're not discriminated against. And we're protected against sexual harassment by law. And we also have affirmative action. At the moment abortions are still easy to get. There's the no-fault divorce law and access to single-parent benefits which made it easy for women to walk out of an unbearable situation.

However attitudes towards women have not changed much. We only have to look at the recent spate of violence towards women. How people still blame the victims: 'She shouldn't have gone to a nightclub. She shouldn't wear these miniskirts. What was she doing at this time of the night in that place anyhow? etc. etc.' And you look at how few women are actually in higher positions in private and public industry. And what a hassle it is to sue somebody for sexual harassment or discrimination. So between legislation and implementation there is a big gap, and within this big gap there are all these old attitudes still filtering through into the workforce, into the courts, into institutions, and they are still held by a large part of society.

We still have to try to change people's attitudes and we have to be vigilant so that the rights we gained are not taken away from us or watered down. No, it's not all over. It will never be all over. We have to make sure that the next generation will know about it and will continue to be watchful.

Also I think there is something wrong when women of today feel uncomfortable with the word 'feminism' and especially uncomfortable with the question: 'Do you still call yourself a feminist?' Years ago they very proudly admitted it.

INTERVIEWER: Yes, a lot of things have changed since the '70s. How have you felt about having to examine the changes in yourself and the other women?

HELEN: It was one of the most positive and enjoyable experiences of my life. I had always felt there was a special bond between the women of the group and I was surprised how strongly I felt it again. After all these years . . . for the first time I understood the full meaning of sisterhood. I'm also so proud of what these women have achieved. How each one has taken responsibility for her own life, made painful changes and decisions and come out of it as a stronger person. They all are examples of the 'New Woman'.

Notes

In this chapter the women tried to sum up their beliefs about the effectiveness of the women's movement, and many of their comments echo things which have been said in earlier chapters.

The legacy of the group was largely an attitudinal one. The women talked of having gained a concept of personal freedom and power, balanced by a new acknowledgement of personal responsibility. The group had also eradicated much of the fear and ignorance which had been able to thrive when the women were isolated. Agnes talked about consciousness-raising 'politicising millions of ordinary housewives' by giving them a wider context in which to examine their lives. Bernadette said the group left her knowing 'My experience is valid and I'm valid'.

The women's movement has been credited with initiating services and practical support systems for women, and for changing some of the laws which discriminated against them. But Gloria and Helen talked repeatedly about the difference between legislating for equality and raising the consciousness of mainstream society. They pointed out that attitudes always lag behind laws. They were concerned that traditional prejudice, indifference, bureaucratic procedures and their own lack of awareness kept women from pressing for the implementation of laws which had been created in their interest.

Women's liberation never became the revolution some had hoped for. Instead it infiltrated a system which was already under attack on other fronts. Even the women in our group found it difficult to know what share of the credit the women's movement deserved for improving their lives, given that many of those improvements had taken place in a general atmosphere of social change. Jane talked of a process, a ball set rolling twenty years ago which grew and gathered momentum, but no one can remember who gave it the first shove, or what it looked like in the beginning.

The assimilation of the women's movement into the mainstream of society has contributed to its invisibility. Not surprisingly members of the group were concerned that many younger women appear ignorant of the recent history. They don't realise how many rights they take for granted today can be traced to action their mothers and grandmothers took yesterday.

Some in the group felt resentful towards young women who have reaped the rewards of hard-fought campaigns without acknowledging their debt to older women. They also feared that this ignorance could result in losses for all of us, and warned against trusting in the permanence of anything which is not guarded vigilantly.

It was interesting that some of the women had opinions about the next generation which reflected fears they have for themselves. For example, Gloria accused young women of being complacent, of aspiring to marriage as the most important thing in their lives, of not taking up other opportunities. She also stated that her biggest fear is that she will be so contented at home that she becomes complacent herself. Sue regretted more than once her lack of 'involvement', then said she hopes for a new wave of activism which her children could be part of.

It is safe to say that all the women who joined the consciousness-raising group had personal agendas, even if they didn't all know at the time what they were. For some women consciousness-raising was the first step in a process that opened them to wider involvement and sympathies. It was a politicising agent for them. For others it appears that interest in the movement began, and largely ended, with their individual concerns.

Any appraisal of the achievements and failures of the women's movement by these women needs to be understood in the context of their original and highly subjective goals, both for themselves and for the wider movement.

For instance, when asked whether she believed the movement had accomplished everything it set out to, Sue cited the number of women in high ranking public office and business as evidence of a great victory. However Helen took that very same number as an indication of how little the movement has achieved in terms of equal opportunity given that we've been working towards it for twenty years.

Jane, who stated 'I'm a success story', and felt that the women's movement is irrelevant today, may have been persuaded to take that view because she is satisfied with her own accomplishments. Similarly, Rose was no longer interested in a women's movement because her personal priorities have changed.

In retrospect there were some negative aspects associated with the movement. Bernadette regretted that as she saw it, a traditional role was no longer an option for women who would have been happy in one. Sophia felt that early feminist philosophy had created confusion about the existence of admirable 'feminine' traits. Several of the women felt that the movement had allowed itself to be appropriated by people with other than feminist agendas, and that it had sometimes nurtured in women a disabling rage.

The movement was seen by some as being in a 'resting' phase, between periods of high visibility. Helen, Gloria, Agnes and Sophia believed feminism was as important today as it had ever been, though Helen felt we might see more individual action and less of an organised movement in the future, and Sophia felt strongly that the cause had to be taken up by the next generation in order for it to survive.

These women realised that it may have been easier and more natural to work for equal opportunity in a burgeoning economy with free education and full employment than to be up against the play-safe conservatism of a society in economic recession.

It was clear from the women's comments that they felt a strong sense of having participated in an important chapter of recent history and that it was their responsibility, as well as a pleasure, to talk about it. Everyone was grateful for the opportunity to re-establish contact with the others, but the conversation sessions had been something of a mixed blessing, occasions for both pride and disappointment.

Many of the women felt that the interview process had acted as an agent for change in something of the same way that the old consciousness-raising group had done. It had provided them with a catalyst for examining their lives, for taking a kind of inventory.

Several women said they believed their sisters were just as non-judgemental today as they had been in the group, and this had made coming together easier. But some felt less than charitable toward themselves as a result of this forced introspection. Jane and Sue wondered whether they'd somehow let themselves down by surrendering to mellowness. Bernadette, while she was delighted and inspired by the achievements of the other women, initially felt the project 'brought up disappointments' in her own life. However, by the last interview she had worked through to a recognition of her own considerable achievements.

Sophia saw the project as being timed perfectly for 'the big reassessment' of her life decisions, and she thanked us for giving her the chance to understand her present by focusing on her past. Agnes too enjoyed looking at the past with mature eyes. She saw the project as a potent reminder of where she had come from, and of the power of sisterhood.

Helen and Gloria said they were engaged in a continual

process of self-examination and evaluation. Nevertheless, Gloria was grateful that the project had rekindled her spirit and made her 'more alert' to the dangers of complacency.

Of all the women, Rose seemed least disturbed, for better or worse, by the experience. The group belonged to a past which was so different from her present as to be irrelevant, though she did enjoy seeing her old friends again. We can only guess what Rita had felt about the project.

There was always a haziness about the circumstances under which the group finished. This raised interesting questions for us as editors about the way memory works: What do you alter when you try to reconstruct the past? How do you account for different impressions at the time, and how reliable are memories of those impressions when they have been overlaid with years and shifting perspectives?

No amount of shared reminiscence made it any clearer. There seems to have been no ritual leavetaking, although Helen is sure she can remember the last meeting. Maybe it wound down rather than halted abruptly. Maybe it doesn't matter. But we did like the way Sue talked of the group's end, as though it had been a family, which nurtured, educated, prepared and then released. No one seriously suggested resurrecting the group.

5

Conclusion

It has been almost three years since we got the bright idea of documenting the impact of the women's movement on the women in our old CR group. There were a few times when, faced with piles of tape recordings, mountains of transcripts and not much idea of how to organise any of it, we thought we might have taken on more than we could deal with. But whenever we explained what we were doing to people outside the group, the reaction was so enthusiastic that we knew we had to keep going.

Being able to see everyone again was a great gift that enriched us emotionally and intellectually. Revisiting a bumpy past from the relative calm of the present was a luxury. Checking out memories, comparing impressions, correcting misconceptions and particularly reaffirming the bond between us were opportunities of a lifetime.

We never intended to draw conclusions or prove points, but simply to document experience. The interviews revealed as many differences in attitudes as similarities. However, two conclusions are unavoidable as far as these particular women are concerned. First, the CR group fostered a climate of trust and tolerance in which they could learn about themselves and each other. Second, the women's movement, and specifically the CR group, gave them confidence in themselves and support for their life choices.

We were amazed at how quickly and easily everyone slipped back into the sort of comfortable exchanges that had developed during the life of the group. One day Sophia made a comment about the willingness of every single woman to contribute what she could to the project, and we were reminded of an animated series that had been on television years ago. In this story two sisters each had half of a magic ring, and all their lives, when one needed the other she only had to rub her half of the ring and her sister's half would light up. And no matter what distance separated them, they would always answer each other's call.

We realise that sisterhood, like women's liberation, has a quaintly old-fashioned sound about it these days. But sisterhood seems to describe our relationship with each other more accurately than friendship does. What we share has survived distance, difference and time without contact. It's unsentimental, but appears for almost all of us to be unbreakable.

We have said that we never really considered starting the group up again, but everyone felt that it would be good to continue meeting informally. So we have dinner together every few months, and stay in touch with a sort of newsletter that lets people know if something of interest is coming up. We were at one of these dinners recently when Jane observed that if we were just beginning the project now we would probably get a very different book out of it. We suppose she was right, but we are pretty pleased with the one we got.

Bibliography

Personal Interviews, Discussions and Direct Information

Women's Electoral Lobby

21 October 1988: Telephone interview/discussion as a follow-up of a letter dated 6 October 1988 to WEL (with Val Byth).

Women's Liberation Switchboard

26 October 1988: Telephone interview/discussion as a follow-up of letter dated 12 October 1988 to WLS (with Jean Taylor).

Archives of the Women's Liberation Switchboard
(Permission kindly given by Jean Taylor.)

Bon Hull — personal conversation and discussion (Women's liberation activist from the early days of the movement who was kind enough to let us browse through her material which she donated to the Women's Liberation Switchboard.)

Newspapers, Magazines, Journals and Proceedings

The *Age*
The *Age Tempo*
The *Age Magazine* — *Good Weekend*
The *Sunday Age*
The *Australian*
The *Bulletin*
The *Daily Telegraph* (Sydney)
The *Medical Journal of Australia*
The *Herald*
Vashti's Voice
Women's Liberation Newsletter
The Queensland Lawyer, Vol. 9, Pts 1-2, Reports — Abortion (R v Bayliss, R v Cullen), Law Book Company Limited, n.d.

Proceedings — National Women's Conference — 1990, Write People, Canberra, ACT, 1990.

Government Publications

A National Policy for the Education of Girls in Australian Schools, Interim Report of the Commonwealth School Commission, Canberra, May 1986.

Women's Budget Statement 1990-1991, Budget Paper No. 5, in-house version.

Secondary Literature

Clarke, J. and White, K. *Women in Australian Politics*, Fontana Books, Sydney, 1983.

Francome, C., *Abortion Freedom: A Worldwide Movement*, George Allen & Unwin, London, England, 1984.

Grieves, N. and Burns, A. (eds), *Australian Women: New Feminist Perspectives*, Oxford University Press, Melbourne, 1986, reprinted 1987.

Klein, R. D. (ed.), *Infertility: Women Speak Out About Their Experiences of Reproductive Medicine*, Pandora Press, London, 1989.

Lloyd, C. J. and Reid, G. S., *Out of the Wilderness: The Return of Labor*, Cassell Australia Ltd., North Melbourne, 1974.

Roberts, H. (ed.), *Women, Health and Reproduction*, Routledge & Kegan Paul, London 1981.

Rowland, R., *Woman Herself: A Transdisciplinary Perspective on Women's Identity*, Oxford University Press, Melbourne, 1988.

Sachdev, P. (ed.), *International Handbook on Abortion*, Greenwood Press, Westport, Conn., U.S.A., 1988.

Sawer, M., *Sister in Suits: Women and Public Policy in Australia*, Allen & Unwin, Australia Pty. Ltd., Sydney, 1990.

Scutt, J. A., *Even in the Best of Homes: Violence in the Family*, McCulloch Publishing, North Carlton, Victoria, 1990.

Simms, M. (ed.), *Australian Women and the Political System*, Longman Cheshire Pty. Ltd., Melbourne, 1984.

———, *The Women's Charter, Stage 1, The Quest*, Union of Australian Women (Victoria), Melbourne, 1990.

Tuttle, Lisa, *Encyclopedia of Feminism*, Arrow, New York, 1987.

The Authors

Marlene Derlet has a background in linguistics and worked as a language teacher in State and independent schools until 1988 when she was employed as a research assistant at the Koorie Research Centre at Monash University. Her assistance in projects such as the research into teaching Koorie languages in schools and employment prospects of Koorie women has taken her to community and educational facilities in Queensland, Western Australia, South Australia and the Northern Territory. She is also the tutor of the Centre's accredited undergraduate course in Koorie (Aboriginal) Studies. She has a longstanding interest in the education and employment of women and is particularly concerned about the implications of gender-based language and how it influences attitudes toward women.

Kristin Henry has been active in the community writing movement for many years, teaching and organising programs in a variety of contexts, including schools, prisons and community centres. She is particularly interested in helping women to find their voices so that they can tell their stories. In 1989 a Community Writing Fellowship from the Literature Board of the Australia Council enabled her to set up writing workshops with country women throughout north-west Victoria. The following year she became joint Co-ordinator of the newly established Victorian Writers' Centre.

She has published two collections of poetry, *Slices of Wry* (Pariah Press, 1985) and *One Day She Catches Fire* (Penguin, 1992).